Ve

Top Plant-B...

©Cara Green

Forward

I would like to thank you for purchasing this book "The Vegan Diet" and congratulate you for taking the steps to improve your health and wellbeing.

In this book you will find proven strategies to help you find balance in your life by being one with nature. Eating clean, fresh and natural plant-based foods that will not only provide you with the best and purest nutrition but will also reduce your carbon footprint on our beautiful planet and also preserve the natural food chains just as nature intended.

We are going to start by taking an in-depth look of the vegan diet and vegan lifestyle as a whole and how you can easily transition into this lifestyle without feeling like you are missing your meaty lifestyle as well as looking at what you stand to gain by going the vegan route.

We are going to end on a delicious note with some of the best tasting and innovative vegan recipes that will leave you pinching yourself for having not discovered the vegan diet sooner!

If you live by the going green philosophy, this is the book for you!

Enjoy!

Table of Contents

Introduction

"Veganism is not about giving anything up or losing anything; it is about gaining the peace within yourself that comes from embracing nonviolence and refusing to participate in the exploitation of the vulnerable"

~ Gary L. Francione

The Vegan Diet is continually gaining popularity for all the right reasons. However, most people still shun this natural diet as they think it's all about eating bland tasting greens. This beginners diet guide is the perfect introduction to the beautiful vegan lifestyle, complete with the most delicious recipes you'll ever eat without feeling meat deprived.

Whether you are a veteran Vegan or looking to adapt a clean and healthy lifestyle or are looking to transition from a vegetarian lifestyle to a purely vegan lifestyle, this diet guide will hold your hand through the entire process.

We will start by looking at where the Vegan diet all began and how it has grown to be one of the most popular health movements. We will also teach you how to transition gently into the vegan diet without feeling deprived and all the beautiful things you can expect to gain in addition to great health.

Once we are through with all the intricate details of the vegan diet, we are going to jump right into some of the easiest and tastiest vegan recipes that will introduce you to a tasty vegan lifestyle. Do you feel as though you are a carnivorous person? Well, you will be very pleased to learn that we also have vegan meats as you will see from some of our recipes such as vegan gyros and more, which even have the same texture and taste as meat.

You don't need to have any prior knowledge of the Vegan diet and the Vegan lifestyle in general. We will take you through all the important aspects of the vegan diet and most of all, by the time you are through with this book, you will be 100 percent ready to embark on your Vegan journey.

Of all the basic tenets of our lives, health is perhaps the most important. The Vegan diet is one of the healthiest diets stemming from the fresh, natural and wholesome foods that constitute the vegan diet.

Thank you for downloading this book and I hope it sheds more light on the vegan topic and inspires you to make the greatest diet change of your life.

Chapter 1
Evolution of Veganism

Understanding Veganism

In a nutshell, veganism is not a diet, but a lifestyle that completely avoids all animal products and any products that are derived from animals. Extreme veganism goes further to avoid all products that have been tested on animals, including makeup.

This means eliminating foods such as dairy, honey and meat from your diet. The primary purpose of the vegan lifestyle is to restore balance in nature by protecting animals from cruelty and exploitation.

Veganism and vegetarianism are often used interchangeably which is wrong. All vegans are vegetarians but not all vegetarians are vegans. There are different types of vegetarians – vegans, lacto vegetarians (they allow dairy consumption) and ovo vegetarians (allow the consumption of eggs).

In the Beginning...

Veganism is not a modern philosophy. The Vegan Society was formed in 1944 but the vegan philosophy has been in existence for much longer with evidence of a vegan lifestyle dating back to over 200 years ago. But, the real concept of a vegan way of life started taking shape in the 19th century with Dr. William Lambe and Bercy Bysshe Shelley objecting to eggs and all dairy from an ethical standpoint.

In the modern day David Watson brought together common minded individuals comprised of non-dairy vegetarians to discuss the health benefits of their lifestyle and this evolved to what we now refer to as veganism.

Archeological evidence shows that some ancient civilizations made the conscious decision not to eat animals. Pythagoras, the Greek poet, followed what we now call the vegan diet in 500BC as he advocated for showing kindness to all species. Around the same time, Buddha was also promoting a vegetarian lifestyle.

Veganism in actual sense has grown out of necessity especially if we look at the eating habits of westerners. By 2007 Americans were eating a hopping 220 pounds of meat and over 605 pounds of sugar. The escalating rate of chronic lifestyle illnesses therefore comes as no surprise.

There's no doubt that animal based foods are the primary culprits of the current health crisis. Animals today are being restricted from their natural ways of life in the bid to increase their production of dairy, eggs and other products and to also increase their rate of reproduction for economical purposes. The circle of life has been interrupted by the greed of humankind and as we know, when you mess with Mother Nature, all you can expect is havoc.

The vegan diet is based on the sanctity of life. Animals should be left to freely thrive in their natural habitats without the fear of capture by human beings only to be used as guinea pigs or to be forced to reproduce at unnatural rates.

The primary question is; is it okay to confine, raise and breed animals for food and other products, and during their lifetime to feed them with foods that don't make up their natural diet? Meat eaters defend this by saying that animals have no way of knowing the difference but veganism does not agree with that.

The main premise of veganism is to use our control, intelligence and power to drive our planet in a way that does not exploit any animals and to co-exist peacefully and fairly with them.

Veganism is based on a plant based, whole food diet that is centered on purely natural and unrefined whole plants. It mainly focuses on fruits, veggies, legumes, tubers, nuts and whole grains. It excludes all meat – including fish, eggs, dairy foods, animal based oils, refined foods such as refined sugar, bleached flour and anything that can be linked back to animals during its production.

Devoted vegans hold true to their ethical convictions as they advocate for the environment and the increased energy and amazing health benefits they get from following the diet. Vegan foods continue to evolve from simple veggie dishes and salads to gourmet foods and they have also been able to debunk the myth that veganism leaves you nutritionally deficient.

As veganism gains popularity, there is a revamped global movement to treat animals humanely and with respect and more and more people are willingly opting for a vegan lifestyle every passing day.

Chapter 2
The ABC's Of the Vegan Diet

Why go vegan?

Protecting animals is not the only reason for going vegan but for a great number of people, it remains a key factor. Having said that, avoiding animal products is an obvious way to take a firm stand on animal cruelty and exploitation.

Here are some other reasons for going vegan include:

- **Improved health**

The vegan diet is gaining popularity for its immense health benefits, eternal youth, increased energy, younger looking skin, among others. While eternal youth might be a wee bit optimistic, there are definitely many scientifically proven benefits to veganism compared to the typical western diet.

A well planned vegan diet is rich in protein, calcium, iron and a host of essential vitamins and minerals. The natural, plant based sources of the mentioned nutrients are high in fiber, low in saturated fats and are rich in antioxidants, helping naturally mitigate some of the current chronic health problems such as cardiovascular diseases, diabetes, obesity and cancer.

- **Environment**

Living a greener life has never been more necessary. From recycling your household rubbish to walking to work. We are all trying to reduce our carbon footprints and there is no better way than adapting a vegan lifestyle.

How do animal products affect the environment?

Meat production and the production of other animal products places a huge burden on our environment – from the water and crops that are required to provide food for the animals, to all the processes including transport that are involved in the farming and production processes.

The enormous amount of grain feed that's required to facilitate meat production is one of the major contributors to habitat loss, deforestation and extinction of certain species. If we take an example of Brazil, about 5.6 million acres of the land is used to cultivate soya beans which is used to feed animals in Europe. This undoubtedly contributes to the creation of malnutrition in the world by driving poor populations to growing cash crops for animal feed instead of nutritious food for themselves.

On the contrary, considerably lower quantities of water and plants are required to sustain veganism, making a vegan switch easier, sustainable and the most effective way to reduce negative impact on our environment.

The Negative Health Effects of Meat Consumption

We have already established that eating meat not only creates health concerns but it also impacts the environment and the poor animals negatively. Here are some of the ways eating meat can deteriorate your health

- **Meat is not as nutrient-dense as plant based foods**

Animal food products are not as nutritionally diverse as their plant counterparts. With animal based foods, you pretty much get two main nutrients; fat and protein, with very few vitamins and minerals and essentially no fiber.

What you might not know is that your body needs a good dose of vitamins and minerals in order to successfully digest and assimilate consumed protein and fat efficiently. You also need fiber to keep things moving along your digestive tract.

- **High toxic content**

In the simple terms, animals, including us, are sponges that soak in toxicity. Because a larger part of the animals' biological makeup is fat, their bodies can build up an excessive amount of toxins.

So, when animals are fed on toxic feed, these toxins become part of their biological makeup and they end up on your plate, not to mention the amount of anti-biotics and artificial hormones they feed to the animal while they are alive.

Benefits of consuming live plant based foods

- **Clear, supple skin**

Live plant based foods are very rich in antioxidants, vitamins and minerals which do a great job of eliminating toxic waste from your body and hydrating your skin; leaving you with beautiful and younger looking skin.

- **Sleep like an angel**

A plant based diet is friendly to all your bodily functions. The same cannot be said of animal based diets that usually overburden your digestive system meaning you don't get the required nutrition. The vegan diet ensures that your body functions optimally and when it comes to sleep time, you sleep like a baby as your bodily functions operate in the background.

- **Increased energy**

When your body is functioning optimally, thanks to a fresh and natural nutrient dense diet, you are sure to feel energetic with an increased metal focus.

- **Increased metabolic rate**

The vegan diet is exactly what man was meant to eat. As such, everything you eat that is vegan diet works to the benefit of your body including revving up your metabolism.

- **Decreased lethargy**

The vegan diet is the richest natural source of nutrients. This means that every part of your body is going to receive its required nutrition and so they will be no reason for you to feel deprived. The high fiber diet l keeps you full up to your next meal and you don't need to worry about crazy hunger pangs, and the high amounts of water in the plant based food keeps you hydrated all day.

What to eat on the vegan diet

Fruits and veggies - apples, bananas, mangoes, berries, grapes, broccoli, leafy greens, carrots, variety of berries

Beans and legumes – lentils, lima beans, kidney beans, black beans, chickpeas, etc.

Whole grains – quinoa, rice, whole wheat, barley, rice, oats, etc.

Starch veggies and tubers – winter squash, potatoes, yams, celeriac, yucca, etc.

Nuts and seeds – almonds, cashews, walnuts, flax seeds, pumpkin seeds, hemp seeds, etc.

Superfoods- Cacao, Spirulina, Goji Berries, Maca, Lucuma, Mesquite, Wheatgrass, Moringa

This is definitely not an exhaustive list but the point to note is that the vegan diet is purely based on natural whole foods that have not been refined. A well-balanced diet will provide you with all the nutrition you need.

Avoid all animal based foods and food products including cooking oil and also avoid refined food products that have very little nutrition. The goal here is to eat live plant based foods that are bursting with healthy nutrition.

How to get the nutrition you need

The key to getting all the nutrients you need is eating a balanced vegan diet.

- **Protein**

We don't eat fish, meat, poultry or other animal based foods. These foods are high in protein which is important for our muscles and red blood cells. We need to find the best vegan substitutes that are also very high in protein such as:

Hemp Seeds – at 35% plant based protein with a full amino acid profile, this easily digestible and versatile seed is second to only...

Spirulina – At 65%-75% protein by weight, this is the highest source of protein by weight compared to any other food.

Soy products – edamame, tofu and fortified soy drinks

Whole grains – buckwheat and quinoa

Legumes – beans, lentils and dried peas

Nuts and seeds – almonds, cashews, walnuts, flax seeds, sesame seeds, hemp seed, chia seeds

- **Omega-3 fatty acids**

These are essential for brain and heart health. You can get them from:

Natural oils – flaxseed oil, canola oil, soybean oil, walnut and olive oil, hemp oil

Ground walnuts and flaxseed

Seeds- hemp , chia seeds, flax , sacha incha,

Soybeans and tofu (*organic)

- **Vitamins**

Vitamins B12 and vitamin D help keep your blood cells and nerves healthy and also help your body absorb calcium. You can get these from:

Fortified vegan meat alternatives

Fortified drinks made from almonds, rice and soy

Red star nutritional yeast

- **Minerals**

Calcium, zinc, iron and other minerals are all very important for healthy and strong bones, a strong immunity and generally well-functioning body. You can get a healthy dose of minerals from:

Legumes, fresh fruits, sesame seeds, blackstrap molasses, fortified drinks, dried fruit such as prunes and whole grains.

Knowledge is key when getting into a vegan lifestyle. You need to know the right foods to eat and how to prepare great tasting meals. We are now going to look at some easy and tasty vegan recipes that will jumpstart you on the vegan lifestyle.

Is there anything like ethical meat?

Many of us are tempted to believe that the meat we are eating is ethical and that the animals in question lived a happy and fulfilling life and that they experienced no fear of pain when they were being slaughtered. But, the sad truth is that all living creatures – even free range and including humans, fear death. No matter how good the animals are treated when they are still alive, when it comes down to the matter, they all experience the chilling fear of death.

Light at the end of the tunnel

The great news is that there is always something you can do about it. Every time you go shopping or when you eat out in a restaurant and every time you eat, you can choose to help these animals by leaving out anything that comes from animals.

When you make the vegan switch, you are standing up for all farmed animals including those that are used in scientific experiments. You are making the world a better place and when we all join up, we will restore the lost balance in our world!

Chapter 3
Meal Plans

You've heard it said; 'failure to plan is planning to fail.' Whether you are only cooking for one or for your entire family, taking the time to sit and plan for what you are going to eat for the coming week will not just save you time, money and effort; it will also enhance your healthy eating habits.

Four reasons why you should have a meal plan:

- **You will culture healthy eating habits**

The main premise of The Vegan Diet is to eat food that is going to help your body fight off destructive inflammation and also protect you from chronic disease. When you have a carefully set out meal plan, you won't need to resort to ordering takeout as you will have healthy food waiting for you at home.

Habit is second to nature and as you get used to planning healthy meals, you will soon forget about the processed and inflammatory foods that used to slow you down.

- **You become an informed shopper**

The specific ingredients listed in the recipes you are going to make will teach you the healthiest ingredients that you need to buy. Forget about overly processed food that has got no nutritional value, you focus will now shift to fresh, natural, nutrient dense foods.

- **You will save time and money**

When you know exactly what you are going to cook, you will shop for ingredients more efficiently and thus save more money. You won't also have to waste time brainstorming on what to cook as it's already planned.

- **You will eat a variety of food**

Planning your meals will allow you to eat something new almost every day, if not every day, instead of eating one thing all week. If you have a family, they are sure to dig this method and it will give them something to look forward to every day.

First Month Meal Plan

Meal Plan – Week One			
	Monday	**Tuesday**	**Wednesday**
Breakfast	Yogurt Berry Swirl	Protein Toasts in a Jiffy	Almond Banana Power Smoothie
Lunch	Portobello in Lettuce Wrap	Chili Black Beans	Tuna Salad— Vegan Style
Dinner	No-Sweat Brussels Sprouts Salad	Hearty Squash Stew	Vegan-Friendly Pho
Thursday	**Friday**	**Saturday**	**Sunday**
Vegan Scramble	Homemade Breakfast Bars	Vegan Breakfast Sandwich	Dairy-Free French Toast
Wheat Berry and Bean Chili	Sandwich Stacks	Fresh and Light Vegetable Medley	Vegan BLT
"Philly Cheese Steak"	Vegan BBQ Ribs	Raw Pizza Party	Quick-Cook Coco-Curry

Meal Plan – Week Two			
	Monday	**Tuesday**	**Wednesday**
Breakfast	Peanut Butter and Maple Granola	Homemade Yogur	Whole Wheat Blueberry Waffles
Lunch	All-Green Salad Bowl	Creamy Avocado Spaghetti	Sweet Potato and Beet Medley
Dinner	Couscous with Spicy Veggie Tagine	Vegan Meatballs	Asian Steamy Pot
Thursday	**Friday**	**Saturday**	**Sunday**
Berry Breakfast Bars	Granola with a Zing	Make-Ahead Lentil Breakfast Bowl	Vegan Fruit Crepe
Summer Salad	Tortilla and Chickpea Salad	Nacho Cheese Sandwich	Portobello in Lettuce Wrap
Classic Tomato and Basil Pasta	Sweet and Spicy Tofu Chunks	Spiced Coco Rice Noodles	Roasted Sweet Potatoes

Meal Plan – Week Three			
	Monday	**Tuesday**	**Wednesday**
Breakfast	Homemade Breakfast Bars	Sweet Potato Breakfast Casserole	Raspberry-filled Breakfast Muffins
Lunch	Avocado and Lentil Wraps	Deconstructed Vegan Sushi	Thai Protein Bowl
Dinner	Vegan Burgers	Roasted Sweet Potatoes	Healthy Raw Pasta
Thursday	**Friday**	**Saturday**	**Sunday**
Chia Pudding	Homemade Yogurt	Coconut Oats with Blueberry Jam Parfait	Tofu scramble – Ethiopian Cuisine
100-% Rye Zucchini Sandwiches	Fresh Zucchini Noodles	Nutty Collard Wraps	Vegan Sloppy Joes
Baked Potato Bowl	Quick-Cook Coco-Curry	Homemade Hot Pot	Couscous with Veg Stew

Meal Plan – Week Four			
	Monday	**Tuesday**	**Wednesday**
Breakfast	*Tasty Chia Pudding*	*Jumbo Breakfast Pancake*	*The Green Devil!*
Lunch	*Vegan Spaghetti Bolognaise*	*Deconstructed Vegan Sushi*	*Sandwich Stacks*
Dinner	*Vegan BBQ Ribs*	*Peanut Sauce on Soba*	*Yummy Rawzania*
Thursday	**Friday**	**Saturday**	**Sunday**
Raw Beet Granola	*Apples n' Oats*	*Veggie Hash*	*Raspberry-filled Breakfast Muffins*
Chili Black Beans	*Curried Pumpkin Soup*	*Veggie Stew*	*Collard Greens and Garbanzo Soup*
Vegan Shepherd's Pie	*Red Peppers and Roast Almonds Penne*	*Chick Peas, Chards, and Tomato Roast*	*Black Beans on Rice*

Second Month Meal Plan

	Meal Plan – Week One		
	Monday	**Tuesday**	**Wednesday**
Breakfast	Sautéed Veggies on Hot Bagels	Coco-Tapioca Bowl	Crispy Pancake Oats with Berries and Almonds
Lunch	Rosemary and Garlic Infused Nutty Cheese	Pregnant Sweet Potato	Creamy Broccoli Pasta
Dinner	White Bean and Avocado Club Sandwich	Sweet and Spicy Tofu Chunks	Vegan-Friendly Pho
Thursday	**Friday**	**Saturday**	**Sunday**
Protein Toasts in a Jiffy	Granola with a Zing	Berry Breakfast Bars	Vegan Fruit Crepe
Creamy Avocado Spaghetti	Nacho Cheese Sandwich	Pesto Bean Soup	Tortilla and Chickpea Salad
Classic Tomato and Basil Pasta	Homemade Vegan Pizza	Crispy "Steak:	Spinach Soup with Bowtie Pasta

		Meal Plan – Week Two	
	Monday	**Tuesday**	**Wednesday**
Breakfast	Whole Wheat Blueberry Waffles	Veggie Hash	Vegan Bacon
Lunch	Chickpea Curry Salad	Fresh and Light Vegetable Medley	Nutty Collard Wraps
Dinner	Hot Chickpea Sliders	Hearty Squash Stew	Black Beans on Rice
Thursday	**Friday**	**Saturday**	**Sunday**
Peanut Butter and Maple Granola	Yogurt Berry Swirl	Almond Banana Power Smoothie	The True Definition of a Power Smoothie!
Portobello in Lettuce Wrap	Vegan Meatloaf	All-Green Salad Bowl	Curried Pumpkin Soup
Thai Salad with Peanut Sauce	Homemade Hot Pot	Roasted Vegetable Salad	Roasted Sweet Potatoes

Meal Plan – Week Three			
	Monday	**Tuesday**	**Wednesday**
Breakfast	Protein Toasts in a Jiffy	Crispy Pancake Oats with Berries and Almonds	Make-Ahead Lentil Breakfast Bowl
Lunch	Tuna Salad— Vegan Style	Deconstructed Vegan Sushi	Thai Protein Bowl
Dinner	Raw Pizza Party	Spiced Coco Rice Noodles	Asian Steamy Pot
Thursday	**Friday**	**Saturday**	**Sunday**
Vegan-Friendly Banana Bread	Sautéed Veggies on Hot Bagels	Coco-Tapioca Bowl	Vegan Breakfast Burrito
100-% Rye Zucchini Sandwiches	Cooked Wheat Berries	Vegan Gyros	Cauli Chili Pops
Mushroom and Pepper Fajitas	Spinach Soup with Bowtie Pasta	Eggplant Curry Rice Bowl	"Philly Cheese Steak"

Meal Plan – Week Four			
	Monday	**Tuesday**	**Wednesday**
Breakfast	Choco-Banana Oats	Raw Beet Granola	Tofu scramble – Ethiopian Cuisine
Lunch	Vegan Meatloaf	Kale and Apple Crisps Salad	Summer Salad
Dinner	Chick Peas, Chards, and Tomato Roast	Crispy "Steak:	Quick-Cook Coco-Curry
Thursday	**Friday**	**Saturday**	**Sunday**
Apples n' Oats	Mango Granola	Crispy Pancake Oats with Berries and Almonds	Sweet Potato Breakfast Casserole
Asian Veggie Salad	Zucchini Pasta	Deconstructed Vegan Sushi	Sweet Potato and Beet Medley
Healthy Raw Pasta	Sweet and Spicy Tofu Chunks	Vegan BBQ Ribs	White Bean and Avocado Club Sandwich

Chapter 4
Breakfast Recipes

Tofu scramble – Ethiopian Cuisine

Note: this recipe is very well spiced without being overly spicy. For this meal, go out to an Ethiopian restaurant for dinner, or order in, and order injera. Save some of the injera for tomorrow's breakfast.

Ingredients

- Left over injera, torn up – this is optional but it makes a huge difference
- 1 huge broccoli floret, finely chopped
- 1 pkt extra firm tofu
- ½ avocado, cubed
- 2 cloves garlic, crushed

Spice mix:

- ½ tsp sweet paprika
- ½ tsp curry powder
- ½ tsp cumin
- A good pinch cardamom powder and cinnamon powder
- ¼ tsp dried thyme
- A dash of ground cloves and allspice
- ½ tsp sea salt or to taste

Directions

1. Sauté the garlic and broccoli in some olive oil on a medium to high flame for about 2 minutes, stirring constantly so the garlic doesn't burn.
2. Add the tofu and cook until it browns evenly, keep turning with a metallic spatula so the tofu doesn't stick. This will ensure that the tofu attains a delicious crunch instead of the crust being left on the pan. Cook for a total of 8 minutes or so.
3. As the tofu is cooking, combine the spice mix in a small bowl and add 2 tablespoons of water and stir well. Add the spice mix to the tofu scramble, stirring well then add the injera. Cook for 2-5 minutes and turn off the heat.
4. Mix the scramble with avocado and serve immediately. Enjoy!

Coconut Oats with Blueberry Jam Parfait

Ingredients

Vegan oats:

- 1 cup rolled oats
- 420ml full fat organic coconut milk
- ¼ tsp cinnamon
- ½ tsp cardamom powder
- 3 tbsp. chia seeds
- 2 small ripe pears, diced, for serving
- 1 tbsp. pure maple syrup

Blueberry jam:

- 4 cups frozen blueberries
- 3 tbsp. chia seeds
- ¼ cup pure maple syrup
- 1 tsp freshly squeezed lemon juice
- 1 dash fine sea salt

Directions

1. Combine all the vegan oats ingredients in a medium jar with a lid and stir well to blend all the ingredients together. Cover the jar and chill overnight for the best results.
2. To prepare the blueberry jam, place a medium, heavy bottomed pot on a medium to high flame and add the blueberries and the maple syrup. Stir in the dash of salt and simmer for 10 minutes until the berries soften and release a lot of water.
3. Stir in the chia seeds, lower the flame and simmer for another 10 minutes until the jam reduces and becomes thick. Turn off the flame and pour in the lemon juice and scoop the jam into a bowl and chill in the fridge for about 2 hours without covering.
4. Remove the oats from the fridge and stir well. Layer the jam, oats and pears into serving glasses. Cover the leftovers and store in your fridge or freezer.
5. Enjoy!

Jumbo Breakfast Pancake

Ingredients

- ½ cup chickpea flour
- ¼ cup red pepper, finely chopped
- ¼ cup spring onions, finely chopped
- ¼ tsp garlic powder
- ¼ tsp baking powder
- ¼ tsp fine sea salt
- A good pinch freshly ground black pepper
- A small pinch red pepper flakes
- ½ cup water
- Avocado, cashew cream, salsa and hummus for serving

Directions

1. Prep the veggies for serving then set aside. Squeeze a bit of lemon juice on the avocado so it doesn't oxidize.
2. Use a whisk to combine the flour, pepper, garlic powder, baking powder, salt, red pepper flakes, in a mixing bowl. Whisk in the water and keep whisking until there are no more lumps and bubbles of air are created – this will make the pancakes fluffy.
3. Stir in the red pepper and green onions then set aside. Place a non-stick pan over a medium flame. Test it out with a drop of water to see if it's hot enough. If it sizzles then it's good to go. Generously spray with olive oil and use a ladle to pour in the batter and spread it out well.
4. Cook for 5 minutes or so until the bottom turns golden then flip it over and cook the other side until golden for about 5 minutes. These chickpea pancakes take more time to cook so don't be in too much of a hurry. Repeat the cooking process with the remaining batter.
5. Serve on a large platter and top with your preferred toppings. Enjoy!

Homemade Pumpkin Porridge

Ingredients

- ⅓ cup almond pulp, (this is what's left over after making almond milk)
- 1 heap tablespoon ground chia seed or flax seed)
- 1 cup canned pumpkin (or homemade pumpkin puree)
- ⅓ cup almond milk (plus extra as needed)
- Pinch sea salt
- ½ teaspoon ground cinnamon
- 2 teaspoons maple syrup or honey/coconut nectar (only if desired, can be substituted with stevia)
- chopped nuts(almonds, brazil nuts, cashews), organic cacao nibs, dried fruit, etc.

Directions

1. Add the pulp, flax/chia meal, pumpkin puree, almond milk, sea salt, and cinnamon to a small sauce pan. Whisk the ingredients together and heat over medium flame until they start to bubble.
2. Reduce porridge to a simmer for a few minutes on low, stirring frequently. Remove from heat and drizzle with maple syrup. Sprinkle with toppings as desired, and serve.
3. Makes a single serving.

Tasty Chia Pudding

Ingredients

- ¾ cup chia seeds
- 4 dates, pitted
- 2 cups almond milk, or other nut milk of choice
- A dash of sea salt
- 1 tsp vanilla extract
- ¼ tsp cinnamon, optional

Directions

1. Combine all the ingredients in a bowl and stir well to combine then let it rest for 5 minutes. Continue stirring after every 5 minutes for a total of 30 minutes until the chia seeds become plump and the pudding acquires a thick consistency.
2. Serve with a glass of coconut water and enjoy!
3. Note: you can reuse the leftovers for the perfect pre-workout snack.

Yogurt Berry Swirl

Ingredients
- 1 cup raspberries
- 2 cups strawberries, cut in quarters
- 2 cups non-dairy yogurt
- ½ cup coconut water
- 1 tsp freshly squeezed lemon juice
- 5 tbsp. chia seeds
- 1 tbsp. maple syrup
- 1 tsp vanilla extract
- Coarsely chopped mixed nuts for serving

Directions
1. Combine the berries, lemon, vanilla, maple syrup and coconut water in your blender and pulse until smooth. Pour this smoothie over the chia seeds in a bowl and combine well, keep stirring in intervals for a total of 15 minutes to make a pudding then chill it in your fridge overnight.
2. Stir the berry pudding before using it then make a swirl by adding half a cup of the yogurt ad half a cup of the berry pudding in a crystal bowl and make a swirl then sprinkle with the chopped nuts.
3. Enjoy!

Raw Beet Granola

Ingredients

- A large beet root, chopped
- 1 cup rolled oats
- ½ cup hemp seeds
- ½ cup sunflower seeds
- 1/3 cup golden berries, cranberries or raisins
- 6 dates, pitted and soaked for 4 hours then drained
- 1 tbsp. coconut oil
- ½ cup water
- 1 tsp cinnamon
- A pinch of coarse sea salt

Directions

1. Blend dates, chopped beet, coconut oil, cinnamon, water and salt until smooth.
2. Combine the oats, golden berries and seeds in a large bowl then pour the blended mixture over them and mix well. Layer a baking sheet with aluminum foil and spread the granola mix in a thin layer.
3. You can choose to dry the granola under direct sunlight or using a dehydrator until crisp and crunchy.
4. Serve with almond milk and fresh berries or over a smoothie for the perfect breakfast or have it as a snack. Enjoy!

Almond Banana Power Smoothie

Ingredients

- ripe banana
- 10 almonds
- ½ scoop pea protein
- ½ scoop rice protein
- ½ cup almond milk
- 1 handful ice

Directions

1. Start by soaking the almonds for a minimum of 4 hours or better still, overnight. This will soften them making them easier to blend. Once soft, strain the almonds and add them to your power blender.
2. Add the other smoothie ingredients too and pulse until smooth. Serve in a tall glass and enjoy a protein packed smoothie.

The Green Devil!

Ingredients

- 3 stalks celery
- 3 bunches kale
- A handful baby spinach
- tbsp. coconut oil
- Pineapple slices to taste
- scoop vegan vanilla protein powder

Directions

1. Combine all the ingredients in your blender and pulse until smooth.
2. Enjoy!

The True Definition of a Power Smoothie!

Ingredients

- ½ cup frozen mango, mixed berries or pears
- large ripe frozen banana
- 1 cup almond milk
- 1 tbsp. hemp seeds
- 1 tbsp. chia seeds
- 6-8 medium romaine leaves
- Dulse flakes, for serving

Directions

1. Add all the ingredients to your power blender and pulse until smooth. Serve in a tall glass, sprinkle with a pinch of dulse flakes and enjoy!

Peanut Butter & Berry Smoothie

Ingredients

- 2 cups frozen mixed berries
- 2 medium-sized frozen bananas
- 2 tbsp. natural peanut butter, heaped
- 2 tsp cinnamon
- cup frozen cherries
- cups almond milk

Directions

1. Add all the ingredients to your power blender but take it easy with the almond milk, adding it as needed.
2. Midway through blending, add the cherries then keep pulsing until smooth then serve immediately. Enjoy!

Raspberry-filled Breakfast Muffins

Ingredients

- ½ cup flour
- ½ tsp. baking soda
- ¾ tsp. baking powder
- ½ tsp. salt
- ½ tsp. nutmeg, ground
- tbsp. cornstarch
- cup soy milk
- tsp. apple cider
- ¾ cup and 2 tbsp. sugar
- 1/3 cup vegetable oil
- tsp. vanilla extract
- 1/3 cup raspberry jam
- tbsp. confectioner's sugar

Directions

1. Set oven at 350F.
2. Sift the dry ingredients (except cornstarch) – flour, baking soda, baking powder, salt, and ground nutmeg into a mixing bowl. Mix well and then create a well at the center. Set aside.
3. In another mixing bowl, combine the cornstarch, soy milk, and apple cider. Whisk well until the cornstarch has dissolved in the liquid.
4. Transfer this mixture into the bowl (inside the well) with the dry ingredients. Add the sugar, vegetable oil, and vanilla extract and mix well until there are only a few lumps in the batter.
5. Scoop the batter into a muffin pan lined with paper cups, filling only up to ¾ of the cups.
6. Using a spoon, spread the butter from the middle to the edges and place 1 tsp. of raspberry jam in the middle. Do the same procedure with the rest of the muffins.
7. Place in the muffin tray in the oven to cook for 20 minutes, or until the muffins are firm at the top.
8. When cooked, transfer the muffins on a cooling rack before dusting with confectioner's sugar. Enjoy!

Dairy-Free French Toast

Ingredients

- 8 slices vegan bread
- cup flour
- cups soy milk
- tbsp. tofu
- 2 tsp. cinnamon powder
- tsp. vanilla extract
- tsp. vegetable shortening
- 1-2 ripe bananas, sliced

Directions

1. Place in a blender the flour, soy milk, tofu, cinnamon powder, and vanilla extract, and mix until smooth. Pour the mixture in a bowl.
2. Dip the bread slices in the mixture, making sure that you dip both sides of the bread.
3. Melt the vegetable shortening in a pan heated over medium fire. Place the bread slices on the pan and cook until golden brown. Flip the bread and cook for a few more minutes.
4. Serve with banana slices on top.

Protein Toasts in a Jiffy

Ingredients

- 4 slices vegan sandwich bread
- 2 cups vegan re-fried beans
- large ripe avocado, sliced thin
- ¼ onion, slivered
- sea salt and pepper to taste

Directions

1. Place the bread slices in the oven and toasted to your preferred doneness.
2. Spread the re-fried beans and top with the avocado slices.
3. Garnish with the slivered onions and season with salt and pepper.
4. Enjoy.

Whole Wheat Blueberry Waffles

Ingredients

- cup whole wheat floor
- tbsp. baking powder
- 1 tsp. all spice
- 1 cup instant oats
- 1 ½ cup blueberries, frozen
- ½ cup applesauce, unsweetened
- 1 ½ almond milk, unsweetened
- tbsp. maple syrup
- tbsp. canola
- 1 tsp. vanilla extract

Directions

1. Sift the dry ingredients – whole wheat flour, baking powder, and all spice into a large mixing bowl. Add the instant oats to the bowl and combine.
2. Create a well in the middle of the ingredients and then add the apple sauce, almond milk, maple syrup, canola, and vanilla extract. Mix until the ingredients are incorporated. Set aside for 5 minutes.
3. After 5 minutes (the batter should thicken), add the frozen blueberries and fold.
4. Heat the waffle iron, spray with oil, and scoop the batter to cook according to the appliance's directions. Continue doing this procedure until you've finished the whole batter.
5. Serve warm and enjoy.

Homemade Breakfast Bars

Ingredients

- ¾ rolled oats
- cup water
- ¾ cup dates
- ¼ cup dried cranberries, chopped
- ¼ cup pumpkin seeds
- ¼ cup sunflower seeds
- ½ cup chia seeds
- 1 tsp. cinnamon powder
- 1 tsp. vanilla extract
- ¼ sea salt

Directions

1. Set the oven at 325F.
2. Soak the dates in the water for at least 20 minutes, or until the dates are soft.
3. Place the oats in a food processor and pulse until you achieve a flour-like consistency. Transfer into a large mixing bowl, set aside.
4. Meanwhile, transfer the dates with the water into the food processor and blend until smooth.
5. Add the mixture into the bowl with the ground oats, along with the rest of the ingredients and mix well using a spatula.
6. Transfer the mixture into a baking pan lined with parchment paper. Make sure to spread the ingredients evenly in the pan using a spatula or wooden spoon.
7. Place in the oven to cook for 20-25 minutes, or until firm.
8. When cooked, allow to cool for 5 minutes before removing from the baking pan. Leave again for 7-10 minutes on a cooling rack.
9. Slice into bars and enjoy.
10. Left overs can be stored in the freezer in airtight containers.

Peanut Butter and Maple Granola

Ingredients

- 4 tbsp. peanut butter
- 4 tbsp. maple syrup
- ½ tsp. cinnamon powder
- ½ tsp. vanilla extract
- 2 cups oats

Directions

1. Set the oven at 325F.
2. In a microwave oven-safe bowl, mix the peanut butter and maple syrup. Place the bowl in the microwave and melt the mixture for about 20 seconds. Stir well.
3. Add the cinnamon powder and vanilla extract in the melted peanut butter.
4. Add the oats and combine the ingredients well.
5. Transfer the granola mixture into a cookie sheet coated with non-stick cooking spray. Spread the mixture on the baking sheet using a spatula.
6. Place in the oven to bake for 7 minutes, or until the granola is lightly brown.
7. Allow the granola to cool before serving in a bowl with a splash of almond milk and slices of banana.

Vegan Breakfast Sandwich

Ingredients

- vegan English muffin
- 1 pc. soy sausage, pressed and formed into a patty
- bell pepper slices
- a handful of baby spinach
- ½ tsp. vegan butter
- 1 tsp. berry jam
- black pepper to taste
- 1 tsp. olive oil

Directions

1. Slice the English muffin into half and set aside.
2. Brush the patty with the olive oil and cook in a heated grill or a covered pan and cook for 2-3 minutes.
3. Spread the vegan butter on one slice of the muffin and place the cooked sausage patty on top and top with the bell pepper slices and baby spinach. Spread the berry jam on the other slice before sandwiching the patty and vegetables.
4. Place the sandwich in a panini press and allow the sandwich to be lightly toasted.
5. Serve immediately, or wrap the sandwich for a to-go breakfast.

Vegan-Friendly Banana Bread

Ingredients

- 2 ripe bananas, mashed
- 1/3 cup brewed coffee
- 3 tbsp. chia seeds
- 6 tbsp. water
- ½ cup soft vegan butter
- ½ cup maple syrup
- 2 cups flour
- 2 tsp. baking powder
- tsp. cinnamon powder
- 1 tsp. allspice
- ½ tsp. salt

Directions

1. Set oven at 350F.
2. Place the chia seeds in a small bowl and soak it with 6 tbsp. of water. Stir well and set aside.
3. In a mixing bowl, beat with a hand mixer the vegan butter and maple syrup until it turns fluffy. Add the chia seeds along with the mashed bananas.
4. Mix well and then add the coffee.
5. Meanwhile, sift all the dry ingredients (flour, baking powder, cinnamon powder, all spice, and salt) and then gradually add into the bowl with the wet ingredients.
6. Combine the ingredients well and then pour over a baking pan lined with parchment paper.
7. Place in the oven to bake for 30-40 minutes, or until the toothpick comes out clean after inserting in the bread.
8. Allow the bread to cool before serving.

Crispy Pancake Oats with Berries and Almonds

Ingredients

- ½ steel cut oats
- cups coconut milk
- cups water
- 1/3 cup brown sugar
- a pinch of salt
- 2 cups berries of your choice
- ½ cup maple syrup
- ¼ cup roasted almonds, chopped

Directions

1. In a large pan, combine the oats, coconut milk, water, sugar, salt, and bring to a boil.
2. When boiling, reduce the heat and allow to simmer for 20 mins until the oats thicken.
3. Transfer the cooked oats in a baking dish and allow to cool for an hour or more.
4. When the oats begin to be cake-like, cut into serving pieces.
5. Coat a non-stick pan with cooking spray and heat over medium fire and place the cut oats into the hot pan. Cook each side until it turns lightly brown.
6. Transfer on a serving dish.
7. Meanwhile, pour the syrup in a small sauce pan and bring to a boil.
8. Pour the boiling syrup in a bowl with your choice of berries and allow to stand for a few minutes.
9. Top the cooked pancake oats with the sweetened berries before serving. And garnish with chopped roasted almonds.
10. Enjoy.

Vegan Breakfast Burrito

Ingredients

- 14 oz. extra-firm tofu
- ½ cup whole wheat flour
- ¼ cup yeast
- ½ tsp. garlic powder
- 2 tsp. onion powder
- ¼ tsp. turmeric
- 2 tbsp. liquid aminos
- 8 pcs. vegan corn tortilla

Directions

1. Drain the extra-firm tofu and transfer into a plate.
2. Cover the tofu with another plate and place weight (around 1lb.) on top and allow to sit for 30 minutes.
3. Allow the liquid to extract and then drain again.
4. Transfer the tofu in a bowl and crumble into smaller pieces.
5. Add the flour, yeast, garlic powder, onion powder, and turmeric with the tofu and carefully toss.
6. Add the liquid aminos and toss carefully.
7. Heat a large non-stick pan over high temperature. Add the tofu mixture into the pan when it is hot and stir to prevent the tofu from sticking onto the pan.
8. Cook until the tofu is almost crispy.
9. Scoop the cooked tofu onto the tortilla wraps and serve with toppings of your choice (ex. salsa).
10. Enjoy.

Vegan Scramble

Ingredients

- 7 oz. firm tofu
- ½ cup dried tomatoes, chopped
- 12 pcs. asparagus, boiled
- ¼ tsp. turmeric
- sea salt and pepper to taste
- 4 slices whole-wheat vegan bread

Directions

1. Place the dried tomatoes in a bowl and pour over hot water. Allow to sit until the tomatoes are soft.
2. Meanwhile, cut the tofu and crumble into smaller pieces.
3. Pour about ¼ cup water into a frying pan heated over medium-high temperature. Add the crumbled tofu, turmeric and season with salt and pepper.
4. Cover the pan and cook for 8-10 minutes, or until the tofu is cooked.
5. Top the bread slices with the cooked tofu scramble, asparagus, and dried tomatoes. Season with salt and pepper before serving.

Make-Ahead Lentil Breakfast Bowl

Ingredients

- cup lentils
- tbsp. green onions, chopped
- clove of garlic, sliced thin
- 1 tbsp. tomato paste
- ½ cups water
- tbsp. low-sodium soy sauce
- salt and pepper to taste
- tbsp. olive oil

Directions

1. Drizzle the oil in a pan and heat over medium temperature.
2. Add the garlic slices, green onions, and tomato paste and cook for about 4 minutes. Stir constantly.
3. Add the lentils into the pan and pour the water. Stir and bring to a boil.
4. When boiling, reduce the heat and allow to simmer for 50 minutes or until the lentils are tender. Stir occasionally.
5. Turn off the heat and let it sit for 10 minutes. Splash with low-sodium soy sauce and season with salt and pepper.
6. Transfer the cooked lentils into bowls and serve, or transfer into an air-tight container and place in the freezer to store for up to five days.

Apples n' Oats

Ingredients

- 2 apples, diced
- pc. ripe banana, sliced
- ½ cup raisins
- 1 cup oats
- 1 cup water
- 1 cup almond milk
- tbsp. maple syrup
- tbsp. cinnamon
- ½ tsp. nutmeg, ground

Directions

1. Set oven at 355F
2. Boil the water and then pour over the oats in a bowl. Leave for 10 minutes.
3. After 10 minutes, add all the remaining ingredients and stir well.
4. Pour the mixture in a baking dish and place in the oven to cook for 30 minutes, or until the oats turn golden brown.
5. Enjoy.

Vegan Bacon

Ingredients

- 5oz. tempeh
- tbsp. tamari
- ½ tsp. hot sauce
- 1 tsp. cumin, ground
- tsp. smoke flavoring
- 1 tbsp. olive oil
- salt and pepper to taste

Directions

1. Using a sharp knife, slice the tempeh thin to look like bacon strips.
2. In a bowl, combine all the tamari, hot sauce, cumin, smoke flavoring, and olive oil and stir. Place the sliced tempeh in the bowl and allow to marinate for 1-2 minutes.
3. Drizzle 1 tsp. of olive oil in a non-stick pan over medium-high heat. When the pan is hot, place the tempeh to cook for 2 minutes on each side, or until both sides are crisp.
4. Place the cooked "bacon" on a paper towel to cool before seasoning with salt and pepper.
5. Enjoy the tempeh bacon with a side of vegan scramble.

Granola with a Zing

Ingredients

- cup oats
- ¼ cup sunflower seeds
- ¼ cup almonds, chopped
- ¼ cup walnuts, chopped
- 1/8 cup dried coconut, unsweetened
- 1/8 cup dried peaches, chopped
- 1/8 cup flax seed
- ½ lime, zested and juiced (about 1 tbsp.)
- ½ lemon, zested and juiced (about 2 tbsp.)
- ½ orange, zested and juiced (about 2 tbsp.)
- 1 ½ tbsp. grape seed oil
- 1 ½ tbsp. maple syrup
- ½ vanilla
- 16 oz. homemade soy yogurt (see next recipe)

Directions

1. Set oven at 300F.
2. Combine all the ingredients except the vanilla soy yogurt in a large oven-safe dish. And place in the oven to bake for minutes. Stir the granola and bake again for 15 minutes.
3. Remove the dish in the oven and allow to cool before transferring the granola in a bowl   and then serving with vanilla soy yogurt.

Homemade Yogurt

Ingredients

- liter soy milk
- ½ cup soy yogurt
- 1 tsp. agar agar powder

Directions

1. Set the oven at 120F.
2. In a sauce pan, combine the soy milk and agar agar powder and stir well. Place the sauce pan on medium fire and heat to 195F (you can use a cooking temperature for this). Make sure the mixture does not boil.
3. Pour the soy milk mixture in a bowl and allow to cool to 105F.
4. Add the soy yogurt into the bowl and mix well.
5. Pour the yogurt into an oven-safe glass container.
6. Turn off the preheated oven and place the jars (uncovered) and leave it there for 8 hours. Make sure not to open the oven while waiting.
7. After 8 hours, cover the jars and place in the fridge to chill the yogurt.

Coco-Tapioca Bowl

Ingredients

- ¼ cup tapioca pearls, small sized
- can light coconut milk
- ¼ cup maple syrup
- 1 ½ tsp. lemon juice
- ½ cup unsweetened coconut flakes, toasted
- cups water

Directions

1. Place the tapioca in a sauce pan and pour over the 2 cups of water. Let it stand for at least 30 minutes.
2. Pour in the coconut milk and syrup and heat the sauce pan over medium temperature. Bring to a boil while stirring constantly.
3. Add the lemon juice and stir and then garnish with coconut flakes.

Choco-Banana Oats

Ingredients

- 2 cups oats
- 2 cups almond milk
- ¾ cup water
- 2 ripe bananas, sliced
- ¼ tsp. vanilla
- ¼ tsp. almond extract
- 2 tbsp. cocoa powder, unsweetened
- 2 tbsp. agave nectar
- 1/8 tsp. cinnamon
- 1/8 tsp. salt
- 1/3 cup toasted walnuts, chopped
- 2 tbsp. vegan chocolate chips, semisweet

Directions

1. In a large sauce pan, pour the almond milk, water, bananas, vanilla and almond extract. Add the salt, stir and heat over high temperature.
2. Mix the oats in the pan along with the unsweetened cocoa powder, 1 tbsp. agave nectar and lower the temperature to medium. Cook for 7-8 minutes, or until the oats are cooked to your liking. Stir frequently.
3. Scoop the cooked oats into serving bowls and garnish with the chopped walnuts, chocolate chips, and drizzle with the remaining agave nectar.

Mango Granola

Ingredients

- 2 cups rolled oats
- cup dried mango, chopped
- ½ cup almonds, roughly chopped
- ½ cup nuts
- ½ cup dates, roughly chopped
- tbsp. sesame seeds
- tsp. cinnamon
- 2/3 cup agave nectar
- 2 tbsp. coconut oil
- 2 tbsp. water

Directions

1. Set oven at 320F
2. In a large bowl, combine the oats, almonds, nuts, sesame seeds, dates, and cinnamon and stir.
3. Meanwhile, heat a sauce pan over medium heat, pour in the agave syrup, coconut oil, and water. Stir and allow to cook for 3 minutes or until the coconut oil has melted.
4. Gradually pour the syrup mixture into the bowl with the oats and nuts and stir well making sure that all the ingredients are coated with the syrup.
5. Transfer the granola on a baking sheet lined with parchment paper and place in the oven to bake for 20 minutes.
6. After 20 minutes, remove the tray from the oven and lay the chopped dried mango on top. Place back in the oven and bake again for another 5 minutes.
7. Allow the granola to cool to room temperature before serving or placing in an airtight container for storage. The shelf life of the granola will last up to 2-3 weeks.

Vegan Fruit Crepe

Ingredients

- ½ cups whole wheat flour
- tbsp. maple syrup or brown sugar
- tsp. baking powder
- 1 ½ cups soy milk
- 1 tsp. vanilla
- 1 tbsp. extra virgin olive oil
- mixed berries of your choice

Directions

1. Combine all the ingredients in a bowl and mix well.
2. Coat a non-stick pan with cooking spray and heat over medium temperature. Scoop 3 tbsp. of the batter onto the hot pan and swirl the pan carefully to cover the bottom of the pan entirely with the batter.
3. Cook for 1 minute on each side.
4. Serve the crepe with mixed berries on top. Enjoy.

Veggie Hash

Ingredients

- 3 pcs. medium-sized potatoes, grated
- ½ cup carrot, grated
- ½ cup baby spinach, roughly chopped
- ½ medium-sized onion, diced
- ½ tbsp. cornstarch
- ½ tsp. chili powder
- ½ tsp. of salt to taste
- olive oil for cooking

Directions

1. In a mixing bowl, combine the grated potatoes, carrot, baby spinach, and diced onions. Season with salt and mix well.
2. Using your hands, squeeze the liquid from the mixed veggies and drain.
3. Add the chili powder and cornstarch into the bowl and stir.
4. Form the hash into patties and fry in a hot pan with olive oil over medium-high heat.
5. Cook for 3-4 minutes or until the hash turns golden brown.
6. Serve warm and enjoy.

Sautéed Veggies on Hot Bagels

Ingredients

- yellow squash, diced
- zucchini, sliced thin
- ½ onion, sliced thin
- pcs. tomatoes, sliced
- 1 clove of garlic, chopped
- salt and pepper to taste
- 1 tbsp. olive oil
- pcs. vegan bagels
- vegan butter for spread

Directions

1. Heat the olive oil on medium temperature in a cast iron skillet.
2. Lower the heat to medium-low and sauté the onions for 10 minutes or until the onions starts to brown.
3. Turn the heat again to medium and then add the diced squash and zucchini to the pan and cook for 5 minutes. Add the clove of garlic and cook for another minute.
4. Throw in the tomato slices to the pan and cook for 1 minute. Season with salt and pepper and turn off the heat.
5. Toast the bagels and cut in half.
6. Spread the bagels lightly with butter and serve with the sautéed veggies on top.

Chia Pudding

Ingredients

- 6 pcs. strawberries
- ½ cup almond milk
- 6 tbsp. chia seeds
- ½ cup homemade soy yogurt
- 3 tbsp. agave nectar
- ripe banana, sliced

Directions

1. In a blender, combine the almond milk strawberries and blend until you achieve a smooth consistency.
2. In a bowl, add the chia seeds, soy yogurt, and agave nectar and stir well.
3. Let the mixture sit for 15 minutes and stir again.
4. Transfer the mixture into a mason jar, cover and place in the fridge to chill for at least 4 hours or overnight.
5. Serve with banana slices on top.

Sweet Potato Breakfast Casserole

Ingredients

- sweet potato, peel removed and chopped
- ripe banana
- ½ cup rolled oats
- cups almond milk
- 1 tbsp. chia seeds
- 1 tsp. vanilla
- 1 tsp. cinnamon powder
- 1/8 tsp. nutmeg, ground
- 1/8 tsp. sea salt
- tbsp. maple syrup

For the topping:

- 1/3 cup pecan, chopped
- ¼ cup brown sugar
- 2 tbsp. vegan butter
- 2 tbsp. flour

Directions

1. Set the oven at 350F. Boil the chopped sweet potatoes and cook until tender. Drain the water and set aside.
2. Rinse the pot used to boil the sweet potatoes and then pour in the milk along with the oats, vanilla, and chia seeds. Stir and bring to a boil.
3. When boiling, reduce the heat and cook for another 6-7 minutes. Stir constantly.
4. Mash the cooked sweet potatoes along with the ripe banana in a bowl and transfer into the pot with the oats.
5. Add the cinnamon powder, nutmeg, sea salt, vanilla, maple syrup, stir, and continue cooking on low for another 3-4 minutes. Turn off the heat
6. Meanwhile, combine all the ingredients of the toppings together. Mix well.
7. Pour the cooked oats into a baking dish and spread evenly. Top with the pecan mixture.
8. Place the dish in the oven to bake for 20 minutes. And then set on broil on low temperature for 3-4 minutes.
9. Remove from the oven and serve.

Berry Breakfast Bars

Ingredients

- 3 cups rolled oats
- 2 ripe bananas
- tsp. vanilla
- 1 cup dates, pitted and cut in half
- 1 ½ apple juice
- 1 cup blueberries
- ½ cup walnuts
- 1 ½ tsp. baking powder
- ¾ tsp. cinnamon
- ½ tsp. nutmeg

Directions

1. Set the oven at 375F
2. Pour the apple juice in a small bowl and soak the dates for 15 minutes.
3. In a mixing bowl, combine 2 cups of oats, baking powder, ground cinnamon, and nutmeg. Set aside.
4. Meanwhile, blend together the remaining cup of oats with the ripe banana and vanilla extract.
5. Take the soaked dates and add into the blender. Blend again until smooth.
6. Pour liquid mixture into the bowl with the oats. Mix well and then transfer into a 9x9 baking dish lined with parchment paper.
7. Spread evenly and bake for 30 minutes or until the toothpick is clean after inserting into the berry bars.
8. Allow to cool for 10 minutes before cutting into bars.
9. Serve or store in an airtight container.

<u>Lunches</u>

Cooked Wheat Berries

Ingredients
- 2 cups hard wheat berries (red winter variety)
- 1 tsp sea salt
- 7 cups tap water

Directions
1. Carefully sort through the wheat berries, removing any chaff and stones present then rinse under tap water.
2. Add the berries to a heavy bottomed pot then add in the salt and water. Place over a high flame and cover. Once it starts boiling, lower the flame and cook for an hour. Remove from heat, drain and set aside.
3. Serve hot or use immediately, otherwise:-
4. Allow to cool then chill for up to 2 days or put in your freezer for a month.

Wheat Berry and Bean Chili

Ingredients

- 2 cups cooked wheat berries
- 2 (420g) cans black beans, rinsed well
- 1 can chipotle peppers, minced
- 2 cans diced tomatoes, with the juice retained
- 2 tbsp. olive oil
- 1 ycllow pepper, diced
- 1 yellow onion, diced
- 5 cloves garlic, minced
- 1 ½ tsp cumin powder
- 2 tsp red chili powder
- 1 tsp dried oregano
- ½ tsp freshly ground black pepper
- ½ tsp sea salt
- 1 ½ tsp brown sugar
- 2 cups low sodium vegan veggie broth
- 1 lime, juiced
- ½ cup freshly chopped cilantro
- 1 avocado, cubed

Directions

1. Place a Dutch oven over a medium flame and add the olive oil. Sauté the onions, garlic, yellow pepper, cumin, chili powder, black pepper, oregano and salt until soft for about 5 minutes.
2. Add in the black beans, chipotle, tomatoes, brown sugar and veggie broth and bring to a boil then lower the heat, cover and cook for half an hour.
3. Add the cooked wheat berries and cook for 5 more minutes until heated through. Turn off the flame and add lime juice and garnish with cilantro and avocado cubes.
4. Enjoy!

Nutty Tofu Wrap

Ingredients

- 60g seasoned baked tofu, thinly sliced
- 8 snow peas, thinly sliced
- ½ red pepper, thinly sliced
- 1 large whole wheat flour tortilla
- 1 tbsp. Thai peanut sauce

Directions

1. Start by spreading the peanut sauce on the whole wheat tortilla. Arrange the remaining ingredients at the center then fold in the sides over the veggies and roll up to make a wrap.
2. Enjoy!

Fresh Zucchini Noodles

Ingredients

Zucchini noodles:
- 1 zucchini per head
- A pinch of sea salt
- Olive oil, as preferred

Cashew cream:
- 1 cup raw cashews
- Clean drinking water
- 2 tbsp. coconut milk
- Mild curry powder
- Freshly chopped mint to taste

For serving:
- Yellow, sweet, tomatoes
- Baby salad greens
- Fresh cilantro
- Watermelon, mango or cantaloupe slices

Directions
1. Start by peeling the zucchini and use a vegetable spiral slicer to make zucchini noodles. Drizzle with olive oil and sprinkle with a small pinch of sea salt then toss well to combine and set aside.
2. Combine the cashew cream ingredients in a blender and pulse twice to form a crunchy sauce and now move to plating.
3. Arrange the baby salad greens followed by the tomatoes. Serve the noodles at the center of the plate and finish off with the fruit pieces and garnish with cilantro. Serve immediately. Enjoy!

Fresh and Light Vegetable Medley

Ingredients

Veggie couscous:
- 2/3 cup pine nuts
- 2 heads cauliflower
- 2 tbsp. extra virgin olive oil
- 1 tbsp. raw agave
- 2 tbsp. nutritional yeast
- Freshly ground pepper and sea salt to taste

Veggie medley:
- 1 cup cremini mushrooms, diced
- 1 cup fresh corn
- 1 cup zucchini, diced
- 1 cup fava beans, peeled
- 1 cup carrots, diced finely
- 2 tbsp. extra virgin olive oil
- 2 tbsp. freshly minced basil
- 1 tbsp. freshly squeezed lemon juice
- ¼ cup freshly minced parsley
- Freshly ground pepper and salt to taste

Sauce:
- ¼ cup freshly squeezed lemon juice
- ½ cup nama shoyu
- 3 tbsp. raw agave
- 1 tbsp. extra virgin olive oil

Directions
1. Combine all the ingredients of the veggie medley in a large bowl and toss well to combine then set aside.
2. Next blend all the sauce ingredients in until well emulsified and smooth.
3. Now toss the couscous with the medley mixture in the large bowl.
4. Serve into individual serving bowls and drizzle with sauce and you are ready to eat. Enjoy~

Nutty Collard Wraps

Ingredients
- 4 good quality collard leaves
- 1 cup pecans, raw
- 1 ripe avocado, sliced
- 75g alfalfa sprouts
- 1 red pepper, sliced
- ½ lemon
- 1 tsp extra virgin olive oil
- 1 tsp cumin
- ½ tsp grated ginger
- 1 tbsp. tamari

Directions
1. Cut off the stems from the collard leaves and rinse them under running water to remove any grit. Soak them in warm water with the juice of half a lemon for about 10 minutes then dry the leaves using paper towels.
2. Shave of the central root so the leaves become easier to roll.
3. Add the nuts, cumin, and tamari, ginger and olive oil to your food processor and pulse until the mixture forms a ball-like shape.
4. Spread out the collard leaves and divide the pecan mix among the leaves. Top with sliced red pepper, avocado, alfalfa sprouts and drizzle lime juice on top.
5. Fold the top and bottom parts then roll up the sided. Slice the wrap in two, if desired and serve immediately. Enjoy!

100-% Rye Zucchini Sandwiches

Serves 2

Ingredients

- 2 rye sandwich rolls (preferably 100%)
- 2 zucchini, cut lengthwise into 1/2"-thick strips
- 4 cloves garlic, sliced
- tablespoon balsamic vinegar
- 1 cup rinsed white kidney beans
- 1 large roasted red pepper
- 6–9 fresh basil leaves
- 1/2 teaspoon freshly cracked black pepper

Directions

1. Over medium to high heat, sauté the zucchini strips for about 1 minute (try not overcrowd the pan).
2. Reduce the heat to medium.
3. Add the garlic and balsamic vinegar and stir immediately.
4. Sauté this for about 30 seconds and remove from the heat.
5. Blend the white beans and roasted red pepper. Until they puree
6. Toast Rye buns (if desired)
7. Spread the pureed beans on the bottom bun, then add the basil, then the zucchini, and finish off with a garnish of salt & black pepper.
8. Enjoy!

Vegan Gyros

Ingredients

Seitan:

- 450g seitan, shaved
- tbsp. coconut oil
- cloves garlic, minced
- tsp oregano, dried
- A good pinch nutmeg
- A good pinch cinnamon
- A good pinch cayenne

Sauce:

- medium cucumber, peeled and grated
- cup vegan yogurt, unsweetened
- tbsp. freshly squeezed lemon juice
- 1 tsp oregano, dried
- 1 tsp dill weed, dried
- Turbinado sugar, to taste
- A good pinch sea salt
- Freshly ground black pepper

Sandwich:

- lettuce head, roughly shredded
- ripe tomatoes, diced
- 6 pcs pita bread
- pearl onion, diced

Directions

1. Grate the peeled cucumber and put it in a strainer over your sink for 10 minutes, for it to lose excess water.
2. Now, place the strained cucumber in a medium bowl and combine with the other sauce ingredients. Stir well until well blended then cover the bowl with cling wrap and chill in the fridge for 30 minutes to an hour for the flavors to blend.
3. Meanwhile, pour the oil in a skillet over medium heat and sauté the seitan and garlic until the seitan starts browning. Stir in the remaining seitan ingredients and sauté until fragrant and well-cooked then remove from heat.
4. Warm the pita bread then assemble your sandwich by layering the lettuce, onions, tomatoes, seitan and top with the sauce. Tuck in and enjoy!

Vegan Spaghetti Bolognaise

Ingredients

- 450g whole wheat spaghetti
- 400g crushed tomatoes
- cup low sodium vegetable broth
- 115g tomato paste
- 1 cup textured vegetable protein
- tbsp. soy sauce, low sodium
- 1 carrot, diced
- cloves garlic, minced
- 1 onion, chopped
- 1 tbsp. thyme
- 1 tbsp. basil
- 2 cloves garlic
- 1 bay leaf
- 1 tbsp. oregano
- Dry Italian seasonings
- 2 tbsp. nutritional yeast
- ½ cup fresh basil, chopped
- 2 tbsp. olive oil

Directions

1. Place a large Dutch oven over medium heat and pour in the olive oil. Sauté the carrots and onions for about 5 minutes until they start softening.
2. Add a little pinch of salt and all spice; now stir in Italian seasonings and the herbs. Add a bit of olive oil if the pan starts drying out. Add the garlic and stir constantly until fragrant then pour in the vegetable protein. Stir until all the vegetables are evenly coated.
3. Add in the soy sauce which will give the veggies a beautiful dark color and flavor. Next stir in the broth and let simmer for 2 minutes then add the tomato paste and the crushed tomatoes. Lower the heat and let simmer for 10 minutes
4. Meanwhile, cook the spaghetti according to package instructions then drain and serve in a large bowl. Pour the bolognaise on top and garnish with the chopped basil. Enjoy!

Vegan Meatloaf

Ingredients

Meat loaf:

- potato, shredded
- cup quick oats
- cups lentils, cooked
- 1 cup tomato sauce
- 1 onion, finely chopped
- 1 cup celery, finely chopped
- 1 tbsp. ground flaxseed
- 1 tbsp. minced garlic
- tbsp. warm water
- 1tbsp olive oil
- 1 tbsp. fresh rosemary, chopped
- 1 tbsp. fresh thyme, chopped
- ½ cup parsley, chopped

Glaze:

- ¼ tsp smoked paprika
- 2 tbsp. ketchup

Directions

1. Preheat your oven to 350 degrees Fahrenheit
2. Combine the water with the ground flaxseed in a mug and set aside.
3. Pour the olive oil in a skillet and place over medium heat. Sauté the celery and onion and lightly season with salt and pepper of choice. Cook until tender then add in the garlic and cook until fragrant then turn off the heat.
4. Now, combine all the meat loaf ingredients including the flaxseed mixture, seasoning as desired. Mix well to ensure all ingredients are well combined.
5. Lightly grease a loaf pan and scoop the loaf mixture into the pan.
6. Combine the paprika and ketchup in a small bowl and brush it over the meatloaf.
7. Place the pan in the oven and bake for 50 minutes until well browned. Remove from oven and let cool for 5-10 minutes before removing the loaf from the pan and slicing it up. Enjoy!

Chili Black Beans

Ingredients

- 1 white onion, diced
- Water
- 2 cloves garlic, minced
- 16 ounces cooked and rinsed black beans
- 8 ounces crushed fire-roasted tomatoes
- 1/4 cup chili powder
- 2 teaspoons ground cumin
- 1 teaspoon dried Mexican or Greek oregano
- 2 tablespoons chopped fresh coriander (cilantro) leaves;
- squeeze of lime

Directions

1. Over medium-high heat, sauté the onion until most of the pieces are significantly browned.
2. Add a thin layer of water and quickly stir the onion.
3. Let the onion sit and the water evaporate.
4. Repeat this process two to four more times to grow the onion flavour(more time the stronger the flavour)
5. Reduce the heat to medium.
6. Add the garlic and sauté for 1 minute.
7. Add the black beans, fire-roasted tomatoes, chili powder, cumin, and oregano, mixing everything together.
8. Simmer for at least 5 minutes.
9. Hint: This recipe works best in a wok.

Vegan Sloppy Joes

Ingredients

- cup French lentils
  - stalks celery, finely chopped
- 750ml tomato sauce
- ½ (red, yellow)peppers, diced
- 1 pearl onion, chopped
- 1 tbsp. olive oil
  - tbsp. tomato paste
- 2 tsp balsamic vinegar
- 1 tsp cumin
- 1tsp Sriracha sauce
- 1 tsp chili powder
- 1tsp sea salt
- 6 sprouted grain buns, cut in half

Optional toppings:

- Avocado
- Relish
- Coleslaw
- Pickles
- Onions

Directions

1. Pour olive oil in a heavy bottomed stock pot over medium heat and sauté the onion, celery and peppers for 5 minutes, stirring occasionally. Add the chili and cumin and cook for another minute.
2. Now add the lentils, tomato paste, tomato sauce, sriracha and 3 cups of water. Bring the pot to a boil then simmer for 30 minutes, uncovered. If the level of water goes down below the lentils add some more and cook until tender. Once the water reduces, stir in the balsamic vinegar and salt.
3. Serve the lentils on the bottom bun and top with your fav toppings. Add the top bun, tuck in and enjoy!

Rosemary and Garlic Infused Nutty Cheese

Ingredients

- 1 cup cashew nuts
- 1 cup pine nuts
- 1 tbsp. sun dried tomatoes
- 3 tbsp. whole rosemary
- 2 cloves garlic, chopped
- The juice of 1 lemon
- 2 tbsps. almond oil or other nut oil
- 1 cup water
- Fine sea salt and freshly ground pepper to taste

Directions

1. Soak the nuts for up to 12 hours then combine all ingredients in your blender or processor and pulse until very smooth. Adjust the taste, if so desired by adding either salt or amount of spices and pepper.
2. Now line a colander with a cheesecloth or thin kitchen towel then place over a bowl. Pour the cheese mix into the colander and leave it to strain slowly for 2 days as it ferments in a warm place. Once ready, transfer to your fridge for another day.
3. If you want a crust, pop it in your dehydrator for 30 minutes under low temperature.
4. Serve with crackers. Enjoy!

Asian Veggie Salad

Ingredients

- 2 pcs. cucumbers
- carrot, peeled
- 1/3 cup quinoa, dry
- 1 cup edamame, shelled
- 1/3 cup scallions, sliced

For dressing:

- ¼ cup water
- 3 tbsp. all-natural peanut butter
- ½ tbsp. low-sodium soy sauce
- 1 tsp. rice wine vinegar
- 1 tsp. agave nectar
- 1 tbsp. olive oil
- 1 tbsp. sesame oil
- 1 clove of garlic, minced
- ½ tsp. sea salt
- 1/8 tsp. pepper

Directions

1. Cook the quinoa according to package instructions. Fluff the quinoa after cooking.
2. Cut the carrot and cucumber using a mandolin or a spiralizer and place in a salad bowl.
3. Add the fluffed quinoa in the bowl along with the shelled edamame and scallions. Toss to mix the ingredients together.
4. Meanwhile, combine in a blender all the ingredients for the dressing and blend until smooth.
5. Drizzle the prepared dressing over the vegetable salad and carefully toss making sure that the veggies are coated with the dressing.

Thai Protein Bowl

Ingredients

- 2 cups mixed leafy green vegetables of your choice
- ¼ cup cooked tempeh
- (soak cubes in 2 tbsp. tamari, 1tsp. sesame oil, 1 tbsp. rice vinegar)
- 1/3 cup cooked quinoa
- ¼ cup cabbage, shredded
- ¼ cup sweet potato, roasted
- ½ cup avocado, chopped
- ¼ cup bell pepper, chopped
- 2 tbsp. olive oil

For the sauce:

- tbsp. coconut milk
- tbsp. nut butter
- ½ tbsp. tamari
- 1 tsp. rice vinegar
- ½ tsp. red curry paste

Directions

1. Cook the quinoa according to package instructions. Set aside.
2. Heat the olive oil on a non-stick pan over medium heat. When the oil is hot, cook the marinated tempeh cubes for 10 minutes, or until the tempeh turns golden brown.
3. Make the sauce by whisking all the ingredients together in a bowl.
4. In a serving bowl, place the green leafy veggies at the bottom, top with the cooked quinoa, followed by the cooked tempeh, and drizzle over the sauce.
5. Enjoy.

Tortilla and Chickpea Salad

Ingredients

- 15 oz. can chickpeas, rinsed and drained
- tbsp. coconut oil
- ¼ tsp garlic powder
- 1/8 tsp. salt
- 4 tbsp. hot sauce
- 1 bunch kale, stemmed and chopped
- 4 pcs. vegan tortilla wrap

For dressing:

- ¼ cup hummus
- 2 tbsp. maple syrup
- 3 tbsp. lemon juice
- 2 tbsp. hot water

Directions

1. Combine all the ingredients of the dressing in a small bowl and whisk. Set aside.
2. Place the chopped kale on a salad bowl and drizzle with prepared dressing. Toss.
3. Prepare the chickpeas by combining it in a bowl with the melted coconut oil, hot sauce and season with garlic powder and salt. Toss the ingredients together.
4. Place a skillet over medium heat and add the seasoned chickpeas. Cook for 4-5 minutes while mashing the chickpeas. One the chickpeas is almost dry, turn off the heat and add a few dashes of hot sauce. Stir and set aside.
5. Arrange the tortillas. Lay the kale on top of the tortilla wrap and scoop the cooked chickpeas on top of the kale. Roll into a tortilla and serve.
6. Leftovers can be stored in the fridge for up to 3 days.

Pesto Bean Soup

Ingredients

- 2 carrots, diced
- onion, chopped
- 15 oz. chickpeas, rinsed and drained
- 15 oz. kidney beans, rinsed and drained
- 15 oz. cannellini beans, rinsed and drained
- ½ tomatoes, diced
- cups water
- 1 clove of garlic, minced
- tbsp. pine nuts, chopped
- 1 tbsp. olive oil
- 1/4 cup extra virgin olive oil
- 1 cup parsley, chopped
- salt and pepper to taste

Directions

1. Heat the olive oil in a sauce pan over medium-high temperature. Sauté the onions for 2 minutes and add the carrots. Cook for another 5 minutes, or until the carrots are tender.
2. Add the tomatoes, water, and season with salt and pepper. Bring to a boil
3. Add the chickpeas and beans and cook for 4-5 minutes.
4. Prepare the pesto by combining the minced garlic, pine nuts, ¼ cup olive oil, parsley, and a pinch of salt and pepper. Whisk well.
5. Serve the soup into serving bowls and top with the pesto sauce.

All-Green Salad Bowl

Ingredients

- ½ cup cooked quinoa
- tbsp. pepitas
- 1 cup arugula
- 1 cup brussels sprouts, sautéed
- ½ avocado, sliced
- 1 tbsp. tahini
- salt and pepper to taste

Directions

1. Combine all the ingredients (except tahini) in a salad bowl.
2. Drizzle with tahini, season with salt and pepper, and toss. Serve immediately.

Chickpea Curry Salad

Ingredients

- 30oz. chickpeas, drained and rinsed
- ½ cup scallions, chopped
- bell pepper, chopped
- ½ cup cilantro, chopped
- ½ cup raisins
- ¼ cup cashews, chopped

For the dressing:

- 3 tbsp. tahini
- 2 tbsp. water
- 2 tbsp. lemon juice
- 2 tsp. apple cider vinegar
- ½ tbsp. extra virgin olive oil
- tbsp. maple syrup
- 1 tsp. turmeric
- 1 tbsp. curry powder
- salt and pepper to taste

Directions

1. Combine all the ingredients for the dressing in a small bowl and whisk.
2. Add all the remaining ingredients in a salad bowl, drizzle with the dressing and toss the salad carefully.
3. Serve immediately.

Deconstructed Vegan Sushi

Ingredients

- cup short grain rice
- tbsp. rice vinegar
- pc. cucumber
- 1 pc. carrot
- 1 pc. avocado
- 1 pc. mango
- scallions, chopped
- 1 pc. nori sheet
- 1 cup edamame, shelled
- tsp. sesame seeds
- light soy sauce

Directions

1. Cook the rice according to package directions.
2. After cooking the rice, transfer in a bowl and pour the rice vinegar over it. Stir until the rice becomes sticky.
3. Julienne the vegetable or use a mandolin to cut the pieces. Cut the seaweed into small strips.
4. Top the rice bowl with the sliced veggies and seaweed, garnish with sesame seeds, and serve with light soy on the side.
5. Serve immediately and enjoy.

Pregnant Sweet Potato

Ingredients

- 2 pcs. sweet potatoes
- can black beans, rinsed and drained
- 1 bunch kale, stemmed and chopped
- 1 clove of garlic, minced
- 1/3 cup water
- 1 tbsp. olive oil
- salt and pepper to taste

Directions

1. Set oven at 275F.
2. Poke holes into the sweet potatoes and place on a baking sheet lined with parchment paper. Bake in the oven to cook for at least 45 minutes to an hour or until the sweet potatoes are tender.
3. Drizzle the olive oil on a sauce pan and heat over medium temperature.
4. Sauté the garlic and add the chopped kale to the pan.
5. Add water and cover and allow to cook for 5 minutes.
6. Remove the lid and toss. Lower the heat and allow to cook for 15 minutes.
7. Add the black beans into the saucepan and season with salt and pepper.
8. Cut the baked sweet potatoes in half, scoop a shallow pit in the middle of the baked potatoes, and top with the cooked black beans and kale.
9. Enjoy.

Sandwich Stacks

Ingredients

- vegan bread slices
- ½ avocado, sliced thin
- 2 pcs. tomato slices
- 2 tbsp. hummus
- lettuce
- 1/8 tsp. red pepper flakes
- salt and pepper to taste

For the pesto:

- 2 tbsp. water
- 2 tbsp. olive oil
- 2 tbsp. lemon juice
- clove of garlic
- 1 cup fresh basil leaves
- 6 pcs. sundried tomatoes
- ¼ cup hemp seeds
- ¼ tsp. sea salt
- pepper to taste

Directions

1. Combine all the ingredients for the pesto in a food processor and blend until smooth.
2. Place the vegan bread slices in the oven and toast.
3. Spread the hummus on one bread slice and then the prepared pesto on the other.
4. Add the tomato slice on top of the pesto, and the avocado on the hummus, stack the bread slices together to create a sandwich.
5. Cut in half and enjoy.

Tuna Salad—Vegan Style

Ingredients

- cup raw almonds, soaked in water for at least 6 hours
- pc. celery, chopped fine
- pcs. scallions, chopped fine
- 1 clove of garlic, minced
- tbsp. vegan mayo
- 1 tsp. mustard
- tsp. lemon juice
- ¼ tsp sea salt
- black pepper to taste
- lettuce
- vegan bread slices

Directions

1. Drain the almonds and place in a food processor. Blend until they're finely chopped (you should achieve a look of a flaked tuna).
2. In a bowl, combine the celery, scallions, garlic, mayo, mustard, and lemon juice and stir well. Add a dash of salt and pepper to season.
3. Lay lettuce on top of the bread slices and scoop the "tuna" spread on top.
4. The tuna spread can be stored in the fridge for 3 days.

good!

Avocado and Lentil Wraps

Ingredients

- 8 pcs. vegan tortilla wraps
- 2 ripe mangoes, chopped
- ½ onion, chopped
- 2 pcs. tomatoes, sliced

For the filling:

- 2 cup lentils
- 2 cups vegetable broth
- onion, finely chopped
- cloves of garlic, minced
- ½ tsp oregano
- ½ tsp paprika
- ¼ tsp. chili flakes
- 1 tsp. cumin
- tsp. chili powder
- 1 tbsp. olive oil
- salt and pepper to taste

For the sauce

- 2 pc avocados
- 1 cup cilantro
- 1 tbsp. lime juice
- ½ cup water
- 1 clove of garlic
- 1 tbsp. agave nectar
- salt to taste

Directions

1. Make the filling by heating 1 tbsp. olive oil in a saucepan over medium heat. Add the chopped onion and minced garlic and sauté for 2 minutes. Add the oregano, paprika, and chili flakes and cook for another 2 minutes.
2. Add the lentils and pour the broth in the saucepan, cover, and allow to simmer for 10 minutes or until the liquid is absorbed. Turn off the heat and season with salt and pepper. Set aside.
3. Prepare the sauce. Combine all the ingredients in a food processor and blend until smooth.
4. Warm the tortillas in the oven and assemble the tacos by spreading the lentils on top followed by the chopped

mangoes, onions, and sliced tomatoes. Drizzle with the sauce and serve.

5. Enjoy.

Vegan BLT

Ingredients

- Cooked tempeh bacon slices
- (refer to breakfast recipes)
- Tomato slices
- Lettuce
- Vegan mayonnaise
- Vegan bread slices

Directions

1. Assemble the sandwich by spreading the vegan mayo on top of the bread slices, top with the lettuce and tomato, followed by the cooked crispy tempeh bacon.
2. Serve warm and enjoy.

Tofu Wraps

Ingredients

- vegan tortilla wraps
- ½ block firm tofu
- ¼ cup red pepper
- celery stalk
- tbsp. red onion, chopped
- ¼ cup vegan mayonnaise
- 1 tbsp. mustard
- ½ tsp. turmeric
- 1 cup shredded cabbage
- 1 carrot, grated
- salt and pepper to taste

Directions

1. Place the tofu in a food processor and pulse until it is crumbled. Add the celery, red onion, and red pepper along with the mayo, mustard, and turmeric, into the food processor. Season with salt and pepper and pulse for a few times.
2. Spread the tofu spread on the tortilla wraps, top with the cabbage shreds and carrots and wrap.

Cauli Chili Pops

Ingredients

- head of cauliflower
- ¼ cup 2 tbsp. cornmeal
- ¾ cup flour
- 1 cup water iced water
- 1 ½ cups sparkling water
- ¼ cup Sriracha
- 1 tbsp. agave nectar

Directions

1. Set the oven at 450F.
2. Chop the cauliflowers into bite-sized pieces.
3. Combine the iced water and sparkling water in a bowl and leave it for a few minutes.
4. Meanwhile, whisk the flour and cornmeal together and gradually add the water. Whisk the ingredients well.
5. Throw in the cauli bites in the batter making sure they are coated with the batter.
6. Place the cauli bites into a baking sheet coated with cooking spray and place in the oven to cook for 20 minutes or until they turn golden brown.
7. Remove the tray from the oven and allow to cool for 5 minutes.
8. Make your sauce by mixing the Sriracha and agave nectar in a large bowl.
9. Throw in the cooked cauli bites in the bowl and toss to coat with the sauce.

Zucchini Pasta

Ingredients

- 4 pcs. zucchinis
- ¼ of an avocado
- 2 cups cashews, raw
- clove of garlic
- tsp. curry powder
- ¼ tsp. cayenne pepper
- 1 tsp. red chili paste
- 1 cup coconut water
- salt to taste

Directions

1. Make the zucchini noodles using a spiralizer. Set aside.
2. Place all the remaining ingredients in a food processor and blend until you achieve a smooth consistency.
3. Carefully toss the veggie noodles in the curry sauce making sure it is well-coated.
4. Serve immediately and enjoy.

Summer Salad

Ingredients

- 2 cups, corn kernels
- 2 peaches, pitted, peeled, and chopped
- 2 tomatoes, chopped
- 2 pcs. scallions, chopped
- clove of garlic, finely chopped
- 1 pc. jalapeno, seeded and finely chopped
- 1 tsp. lime zest
- ½ lime, juiced
- salt and pepper to taste

Directions

1. Combine all the ingredients in large salad bowl and toss the ingredients together.
2. Serve immediately and enjoy.

Creamy Avocado Spaghetti

Ingredients

- 12 oz. cooked vegan spaghetti
- 2 avocadoes, pitted and sliced
- cup cherry tomatoes, cut in half
- ½ cup corn kernels, drained and rinsed
- ½ lemon, juiced
- cloves of garlic
- ½ cup basil leaves
- 1/3 cup olive oil
- salt and pepper to taste

Directions

1. Prepare the avocado sauce by placing the avocados, garlic, basil leaves, and lemon juice in a food processor. Season with salt and pepper and pulse again.
2. While blending, gradually add the olive oil. Blend until the sauce has emulsified.
3. In a bowl, top the cooked paste with the prepared sauce, with the cherry tomatoes and corn kernels.
4. Serve immediately and enjoy.

Nacho Cheese Sandwich

Ingredients

- 3 tbsp. non-dairy nacho cheese
- cup mushroom of your choice, sliced thin
- ½ onion, sliced
- 1 clove of garlic, minced
- 1 tbsp. olive oil
- salt and pepper to taste
- 6 slices vegan bread

Directions

1. Heat the olive oil in a pan over medium heat. Add the onion and garlic and sauté for 5 minutes. Add the mushrooms and cook until it reduces its size. Set aside.
2. Arrange the sandwich by scooping a heaping serving of the mushrooms on top of the bread and top with the non-dairy nacho cheese. Top with another slice of bread and warm in the toaster for a few minutes.
3. Serve and enjoy while hot.

Creamy Broccoli Pasta

Ingredients

- 3 cups broccoli florets
- 6 cups bowtie pasta
- Salt and pepper to taste

For the sauce:

- head of cauliflower, cut into florets
- cloves of garlic
- cup low-sodium vegetable broth
- 2 cups soy milk
- 2 tsp. white miso paste
- ¼ cup yeast
- salt to taste

Directions

1. Prepare the sauce first. Boil the florets, garlic, vegetable broth, and soy milk in a saucepan and simmer for 10 minutes.
2. Transfer into a food processor and blend until you achieve a smooth consistency.
3. Add the remaining ingredients for the sauce and blend again. (store the left over sauce in an airtight container inside the fridge.)
4. Cook the pasta according to the packaging instructions.
5. When the pasta is almost cooked, add the broccoli into the water and cook for a few minutes.
6. Drain and combine together the pasta, broccoli, and the cauli sauce together.
7. Serve immediate and enjoy.

Veggie Stew

Ingredients

- 2 tbsp. extra virgin olive oil
- onion, diced
- cloves of garlic, minced
- pcs. celery, diced
- carrots, diced
- 1 sweet potato, peeled and diced
- 1 pc. zucchini, chopped
- 1 ½ cup vegetable broth
- 15 oz. diced tomatoes
- 2 tsp. Italian seasoning
- salt and pepper to taste

Directions

1. Heat the oil in a saucepan over medium temperature. Throw in the onions and sauté of a few minutes. Add the carrots, celery, and garlic into the pan and cook for another 5 minutes while stirring occasionally.
2. Add the sweet potatoes into the pan and cook for another 6-7 minutes.
3. Pour in the vegetable broth along with the tomatoes into the pan and stir. Sprinkle the Italian seasoning and add salt and pepper.
4. Add the zucchini to the saucepan and cook for another 12-15 minutes.
5. Serve immediately and enjoy.

Sweet Potato and Beet Medley

Ingredients

- 3 cups baby spinach
- 3 cups kale, stemmed and chopped
- pc. sweet potato, chopped
- 4 pcs. cooked beets, sliced
- ½ cup pepitas

For the dressing:

- date, soaked and pitted
- tbsp. extra virgin olive oil
- tbsp. balsamic vinegar
- salt and pepper to taste

Directions

1. Cook the sweet potato on a pan until soft.
2. Prepare your dressing: Combine all the ingredients of the dressing in a food processor and blend until smooth. Set aside.
3. Allow the cooked sweet potato to cool before placing in a salad bowl and tossing it together with the baby spinach, kale, beets, and pepitas.
4. Drizzle with the prepared dressing and toss again.
5. Serve immediately and enjoy.

Curried Pumpkin Soup

Ingredients

- 4 cups pumpkin, skin removed and sliced
- 2 sweet potatoes, chopped
- large carrots, chopped
- cloves of garlic, minced
- 1 tsp. ginger, minced
- 1 onion diced
- ½ tsp. curry powder
- ¼ tsp. coriander
- cups vegetable broth
- ½ lime, juiced
- 1 tbsp. olive oil
- salt and pepper to taste

Directions

1. Set the oven at 400F.
2. Place the pumpkin slices into a baking sheet coated with cooking spray and bake in the oven for 40 minutes.
3. Transfer the pumpkin slices into a food processor and blend until you achieve a puree. Set aside.
4. Drizzle the olive oil in the pan over medium heat. Sauté the garlic and onion for a few minutes and then add the potatoes and carrots.
5. Pour in the vegetable broth and bring to a boil.
6. Allow to simmer until the veggies are tender.
7. Mash the potatoes and carrots and add in the puree along with the remaining ingredients.
8. Stir well and season with salt and pepper.
9. Serve warm and enjoy.

Kale and Apple Crisps Salad

Ingredients

- bunch kale, stems removed and chopped
- 1 pc. apple, peeled and chopped
- 1/3 cup slivered almonds
- ½ cup dried cranberries

For the dressing:

- 2 lemons juiced
- 2 tbsp. maple syrup

Directions

1. Whisk together the ingredients for the dressing in a small bowl
2. Toss all the salad ingredients in a large bowl. And drizzle with the dressing. Toss again.
3. Place in the fridge to chill for 30 minutes before serving.

Portobello in Lettuce Wrap

Ingredients

- 1 lb. Portobello mushrooms
- ¼ cup chili pepper paste
- 1 tsp. onion powder
- 1 tsp. ground cumin
- 3 tbsp. olive oil
- 6 pcs. collard greens

For the guacamole:

- 2 ripe avocados, pitted and chopped
- 2 tbsp. tomatoes, chopped
- 2 tbsp. onion, chopped
- 2 tbsp. lime juice
- 1 tbsp. cilantro, chopped
- salt to taste

Directions

1. In a bowl, mix together the hot chili pepper paste, onion powder, cumin, and olive oil.
2. Brush the mixture onto the mushrooms and allow to sit for 15 minutes.
3. Prepare the guacamole by mixing all the ingredients together in a separate bowl. Set aside.
4. After marinating the mushrooms, heat ½ of the olive oil on a non-stick pan over medium-high heat. Throw in the mushrooms and cook for 3 minutes.
5. Flip the mushrooms and cook for another 3 minutes.
6. Lay down the collard green leaves and scoop the cooked mushrooms on top. Add the guacamole on top and serve by garnishing with chopped cilantro.

Collard Greens and Garbanzo Soup

Ingredients

- ¾ lb. collard greens, steamed
- 2 ½ garbanzo beans, rinsed and drained
- 2 onions, chopped
- 5 cloves of garlic
- 4 cups low-sodium vegetable broth
- 1 cup quick cook oats
- 1 tbsp. olive oil
- 4 tsp. coriander, ground
- salt and pepper to taste

Directions

1. Place a sauce pan over medium-high heat. Drizzle the oil on the pan and sauté the onions and garlic for 5 minutes.
2. Add the coriander and season with pepper. Cook for another 2 minutes.
3. Add the quick cook oats to the pan, add salt, and cook for 2-3 minutes.
4. Pour the vegetable broth and garbanzo beans and allow to simmer for 5 minutes.
5. Throw in the steamed collard greens into the pan and use an immerse blender and blend until smooth.
6. Serve hot and enjoy.

Dinners

Asian Steamy Pot

Ingredients

- 4 ounces bean thread (cellophane) or extra thin rice noodles
- 8 ounces shiitake mushrooms, stemmed then thinly sliced
- 8 ounces green beans, chopped
- 4 carrots, peeled and thinly sliced
- 4 green onions, thinly sliced
- 1 tbsp. extra virgin olive oil
- 6 cups low sodium vegan veggie broth
- 2 tbsp. fresh ginger root, grated
- 2/3 cup low sodium soy sauce
- 1 tsp hot pepper sauce

Directions

1. Cook the cellophane or rice noodles according to package instructions. Drain then cut into bite size lengths.
2. As the noodles are cooking, heat olive oil in a large saucepan over medium flame and sauté the mushrooms for 2 minutes until they start browning
3. Stir in the broth, chili sauce, soy sauce, and ginger then bring to a boil.
4. Add in all the veggies and simmer for 5 minutes until tender.
5. Serve the noodles on individual bowls then ladle over the veggie soup. Enjoy!

Couscous with Spicy Veggie Tagine

Ingredients

- 1 cup instant couscous
- 1 large zucchini, chopped into 1" pieces
- 2 large carrots, peeled and chopped into 1" pieces
- 1 eggplant, chopped into 1" pieces
- 2 cloves garlic, minced
- 1 red onion, chopped
- 2 tbsp. olive oil
- 1 red pepper, cut into thin strips
- ¼ cup golden raisins
- 2 ½ cups vegan veggie broth
- 1 tiny cinnamon stick
- 1 tsp cumin powder
- 1 tsp curry powder
- 1 tsp turmeric
- 3 tbsp. finely chopped cilantro

Directions

1. Place a large saucepan over medium flame and sauté the onions for 5 minutes until translucent. Add the carrots, garlic, red pepper, spices and veggie stock and bring to a boil. Lower the flame and simmer for 10 minutes.
2. Add the eggplant, zucchini, half the chopped cilantro and raisins and cook for half an hour. Sprinkle well with salt and stir.
3. Cook the couscous according to package directions.
4. Serve the couscous and top with the veggie tagine and finish off with the remaining cilantro.
5. Enjoy!

White Bean and Avocado Club Sandwich

Ingredients

- 2 (420g) cans white (cannellini) beans, rinsed
- 120g sprouts (radish, alfalfa, broccoli)
- 1 seedless cucumber, thinly sliced
- 1 pearl onion, thinly sliced
- 2 tbsp. extra virgin olive oil
- ¼ tsp freshly ground black pepper
- 12 slices multigrain vegan bread
- ½ tsp coarse sea salt
- 2 avocados, thinly sliced

Directions

1. Combine the cannellini, pepper, oil, and salt in a large mixing bowl and use the back of a fork to roughly mash the bean mixture then set aside.
2. Arrange 8 slices of bread on a clean surface and equally divide the bean mash among them. Top with the sliced onions, cucumber, and sprouts. Lastly top with avocado and sprinkle with coarse sea salt.
3. Stack the sandwiches on top of each other to make 4 double sandwiches then top with the 4 remaining slices of bread.
4. Slice the sandwiches diagonally if desired. Enjoy!

Yummy Rawzania

Ingredients

- 3 medium zucchinis
- ¼ cup yellow onion
- ½ cup sun dried tomatoes
- ½ cup black olives, pitted and roughly chopped
- ½ batch Italian Pizza Cheese:
    - Juice of 1 lime
    - 2 cups macadamia nuts
    - 3 cloves garlic
    - 1 tsp fine sea salt
    - ½ cup basil leaves
    - ¾ cup water or as needed
- ½ batch sun-dried tomato marinara – recipe below
    - 2 cups tomatoes, chopped
    - 3 tbsp. sun-dried tomatoes
    - 1 tsp dates, pitted
    - 1 clove garlic
    - ½ tsp dried rosemary
    - ¼ cup extra virgin olive oil
    - 1 tsp dried oregano
    - 1 tsp fine sea salt
    - ½ cup fresh basil, roughly chopped
    - 2 tbsp. freshly squeezed lemon juice
    - **Directions**

Sun-dried tomato marinara:

1. Blend all the ingredients apart from the sun-dried tomatoes to a smooth puree. Now add the sun-dried tomatoes and blend until evenly distributed. The sundried tomatoes will make the marinara thick as they absorb most of the moisture.
2. Drain off any excess water so the rawzania doesn't get runny.
3. Store the excess in your fridge and you can also use it as a veggie or cracker dip.

Italian pizza cheese:

1. Blend all the ingredients together until smooth and creamy, adding enough water so it's not too thick and not too runny.
2. You can also use it as a dip or bread spread or even in sauces.

Rawzania:

1. Use a vegetable spiral slicer to cut the zucchini into thin circular spirals.
2. Use a rectangle baking dish to assemble the rawzania starting with the zucchini, cheese, onion, marinara, olives, sun dried tomatoes, thyme and oregano and then repeat the layering.
3. You can eat the rawzania immediately or chill it in the fridge for a day. It tastes better the next day. Enjoy!

Raw Pizza Party

Ingredients

Toppings:

- ½ red pepper
- ½ cup button mushrooms, thinly sliced
- tbsp. black olives, pitted and finely chopped
- 1 celery stick, finely chopped
- 1 yellow sweet tomato, cubed
- ½ cup finely chopped cilantro

Crust:

- cup cashew nuts, raw
- ½ cup fresh basil
- A good pinch kosher salt

Cheese:

- cup cashew nuts, soaked for 12 hours
- ½ cup fresh basil
- 1 clove garlic, core removed
- 1 tbsp. freshly squeezed lemon juice
- A good pinch kosher salt
- 1 tbsp. water

Marinade for toppings:

- tbsp. olive oil
  - tbsp. freshly squeezed lemon juice
- 1 tsp pure maple syrup
- A good pinch kosher salt
- 1 tbsp. water

Tomato sauce:

- cup sun-dried tomatoes, soaked in oil
- 1 tbsp. pure maple syrup

Directions

1. Start by marinating the toppings. Combine all the topping ingredients in a large bowl then mix in the marinade ingredients. Toss well until all the ingredients combine well.
2. To make the crust, add the cashews to your food processor and pulse the cashews into powder form then add in the salt and basil leaves.

3. Remove the dough from the food processor and knead it using your hands for about 30 seconds then press it down on a platter to form a thin crust. Use a spatula to loosen the crust from the bottom of the plate.
4. Next blend all the tomato sauce ingredients until smooth then spread it on the crust.
5. Blend the cheese ingredients and pour over the tomato sauce, leaving some for topping.
6. Add the toppings, spreading them evenly and creatively. Finish off by drizzling the cheese on top of the toppings. Slice up your pizza and enjoy!

Healthy Raw Pasta

Ingredients

- 4 white mushrooms, sliced
- 4 black mushrooms, sliced
- 2 tomatoes
- 10 sundried tomatoes
- 2 cucumbers
- shallot
- 10 dates
- 1 orange, juiced
- ¼ tsp curry powder
- ¼ tsp red chili powder

Directions

1. Combine all the ingredients apart from the mushrooms and cucumbers in your food processor and pulse until you get a thick paste. You may add some water if you prefer a thinner sauce.
2. Pour the sauce over the sliced mushrooms and combine well until all the mushrooms are evenly coated.
3. Chill in the fridge for 30 minutes for all the flavors to meld.
4. When you are ready to serve, use a vegetable spiral slicer to spiralizer the cucumbers into noodles then serve into individual bowls.
5. Top with the mushrooms and drizzle with the sauce. Enjoy!

__Vegan Meatballs__

Ingredients

- ½ cup brown rice, cooked
- ¼ cup nutritional yeast
- 1/8 cup whole wheat flour
- ½ cup vital wheat gluten
- 4 oz. tempeh
- ¼ cup pizza sauce
- 3 oz. freshly chopped spinach
- 2 small cloves garlic, minced
- tbsp. tomato paste
- ½ tsp oregano, dried
- ½ tsp fennel, dried
- ½ tsp basil, dried
- ½ tsp sea salt
- A good pinch red pepper flakes

Directions

1. Start by preheating your oven to 375 degrees Fahrenheit and prepare a baking sheet by lining it with parchment paper.
2. Steam the tempeh over boiling water for about 10 minutes then let cool. Chop it up into very fine pieces then set it aside in a large bowl.
3. Now place a skillet over medium heat and add the spinach and a tablespoon of water. Cook until the spinach wilts then stir in the garlic. Cook for 1 minute then remove from heat. Add the spinach to the chopped tempeh.
4. Meanwhile, combine all the dry ingredients and set aside.
5. Add the tomato paste, pizza sauce and cooked rice to the tempeh and combine well to mix. Add this to the dry ingredients. Don't be scared of getting dirty; use your hands to combine all the ingredients and to form small bowls. You should get about 18-20 balls.
6. Arrange the balls on the prepared baking sheet and bake for 15 minutes on one side then flip them and cook for a further 15 minutes.
7. Remove from oven and let cool for 10 minutes (this step is very important as it ensures your meatballs are firm and not squishy on the inside).
8. You are ready to eat now or if you like, you can stir them in your marinara sauce. Yum!

Vegan Bigos

Ingredients

- 3 cups sauerkraut (reserve juice)
- 3 cups fresh green cabbage, shredded
- red onion, diced
- cups low sodium vegetable broth
- I can chopped tomatoes, reserve juice
- 1 cup sauerkraut juice
- tbsp. tomato paste
- 1 tbsp. olive oil
- ½ cup organic BBQ sauce
- 150g smoked tofu, finely chopped
- 2 vegan dogs, finely chopped
- ½ tsp sweet paprika
- Smoked chipotle pepper
- 1 tsp peppercorns
- 1 bay leaf
- Sea salt

Directions

1. Place a wok over medium heat and add half the olive oil. Next add the onions and sauté them until soft.
2. Now add the cabbage, sauerkraut, sauerkraut juice, stock, tomatoes, tomato juice and the tomato paste. Stir well to combine, cover and bring to a boil until the cabbage mix is just covered by the sauce.
3. Stir in the spices and BBQ sauce and simmer for about an hour over low heat until the cabbage is soft.
4. Meanwhile, add the remaining oil to a skillet over medium heat and sauté the chopped vegan dogs and tofu until they become crisp. Turn off the heat and add them to the simmering pot for the last 20 minute of cook time.
5. Serve immediately in bowls. This recipe goes very well with baked potatoes!
6. Enjoy!

Vegan BBQ Ribs

Ingredients

- cup vital wheat gluten
- ¾ cup low sodium vegetable broth
- cup BBQ sauce
- tbsp. nutritional yeast
- tbsp. peanut butter, natural
- 1 tbsp. smoked sweet paprika
- 1 tbsp. soy sauce
- tsp onion powder
- Fresh black pepper grinds
- 1 tsp garlic powder
- 1 tsp liquid smoke

Directions

1. Start by preheating your oven to 350 degrees Fahrenheit and lightly greasing a baking dish.
2. Mix the wheat gluten, garlic and onion powders, nutritional yeast, paprika and pepper in a bowl.
3. Now whisk the peanut butter together with the liquid smoke, broth and soy sauce until smooth. Pour this over the bowl containing the dry ingredients. Use your hands to knead until you get a soft dough for about 4-5minutes. Scoop the dough into your prepared baking dish and flatten it out using a spatula. Use a knife to create rib shapes by cutting it in the middle lengthwise then cross-wise to form 1" wide ribs.
4. Place the baking dish in the oven and bake for 25minutes.meanwhile, heat up your grill (if you are planning to eat the ribs right away)
5. Remove the ribs from the oven and liberally brush with the BBQ sauce. Place the ribs on the heated grill, with the side with the sauce facing down, and then brush the tops with more sauce. Let the bottom cook for about 5 minutes until they turn deep brown. Flip the ribs over and cook the other side for 5 minutes until they brown beautifully.
6. Serve the ribs immediately with more BBQ sauce. Yum!

Vegan Shepherd's Pie

Ingredients

Creamed potatoes

- 900g potatoes, cut in cubes
- ½ cup Earth Balance margarine
- ½ tsp dill, dried
- ½ tsp sea salt
- A good pinch white pepper

Filling:

- ½ cups yellow onion, diced
- carrots, halved then cut into slices
- Portobello mushrooms, sliced
- stalks celery, diced
- 2 tbsp. Earth Balance margarine
- 2 tbsp. tomato paste
- tbsp. olive oil
- 1 tbsp. rice flour (mix with ½ cup of water)
- 1 cup vegetable broth
- 1tsp sugar
- 1 tsp thyme, dried
- 1 tsp sea salt
- A good pinch freshly grated nutmeg

Directions

1. Place the potatoes in a large pot, cover with water and bring to a boil.
2. Lower the heat and let simmer for 15 minutes then remove from heat. Cover and let stand.
3. Meanwhile, combine the olive oil with 1 tablespoon Earth Balance in a sauce pan then stir in the carrots, celery and onions. Cook for 5 minutes until tender then pour in the stock. Lower heat and cook for 15 minutes.
4. As your veggies simmer gently, add 1 tablespoon to a skillet and put over medium heat then sauté the mushrooms. Add a bit of salt, cover and let cook for 2 minutes. Stir in the tomato paste, sugar, thyme, nutmeg and salt. Cook for another minute then remove from heat.
5. Preheat your oven to 375 degrees Fahrenheit then go back to your potatoes and mash them up but first drain the water. Add the remaining creamed potatoes ingredients then mash.

6. Lightly grease a casserole dish and spread the filling in an even layer. Top with the mashed potatoes, using a spatula to even out and smoothen the potatoes. Use a fork to gently press down on the potatoes then drag. This will give the potatoes texture (some will be more cooked than others).
7. Bake for 40 minutes. Enjoy!

Chick Peas, Chards, and Tomato Roast

Ingredients

- cup wild rice
- 15. oz. chickpeas, drained and rinsed
- 4 pcs. cherry tomatoes, cut in half
- 8 cups Swiss chard, stemmed and ribs removed
- tbsp. olive oil
- cloves of garlic
- 1/3 cup raisins
- 2 tbsp. water
- 2 tbsp. fresh lemon juice
- salt and pepper to taste

Directions

1. Cook the rice according to packaging instructions.
2. Meanwhile, heat the olive oil on a pan over medium-high temperature. Add the cherry tomatoes and cook for 3-4 minutes. Turn the tomatoes on its other side and cook for another minute. Set aside.
3. Lower the heat and then add the Swiss chard, garlic, raisins, water, and season with salt and pepper. Stir and cook for 3 minutes.
4. Add the tomatoes back in the pan and then add the rinsed chickpeas along with the lemon juice and toss.
5. Serve the veggies on top of the cooked rice.

Couscous with Veg Stew

Ingredients

- onion, chopped
- ½ tsp. ginger, ground
- ¼ tsp. cumin
- 15 oz. chickpeas, drained and rinsed
- cups cauliflower florets
- 28 oz. whole tomatoes
- salt and pepper to taste
- ½ cup raisins
- ½ water
- cups baby spinach
- cup couscous, cooked
- tbsp. olive oil

Directions

1. Heat the olive oil in a pan over medium temperature. Throw in the chopped onions and sauté for 5 minutes.
2. Add the ginger, cumin, and season with salt and pepper. Cook for another minute.
3. Throw in the tomatoes into the pan and crush them using a spoon. Add the florets, chickpeas, raisins, and water and bring to a boil.
4. Lower the heat and allow to simmer for 18-20 minutes, or until the soup has thickened.
5. Add the spinach into the pot and then cook for another 2 minutes.
6. Serve the veg stew with the couscous on the side.

Black Beans on Rice

Ingredients

- 2 15oz. black beans
- cup low-sodium vegetable broth
- 1 onion, chopped
- cloves of garlic, chopped
- 1 red pepper, chopped
- pcs. bay leaves
- 2 tbsp. red wine vinegar
- ¼ tsp. cumin, ground
- cups water
- 1 ½ olive oil
- 2 tbsp. olive oil
- ½ tsp. pepper
- salt to taste
- 2 cups rice, cooked

Directions

1. In a pot, pour the water and add a teaspoon of salt and olive oil. Bring to a boil.
2. Add the rice into the pot and cook for 20 minutes or until the rice is cooked through.
3. While waiting for the rice to cook, add the 2 tbsp. olive oil in a pot and heat over medium fire. Throw in the onions, garlic, and red pepper into the pot and sauté for 5 minutes.
4. Add the remaining ingredients and season with salt. Cover with a lid and bring to a boil.
5. After boiling, reduce the heat and allow to simmer for another 10 minutes.
6. Remove the bay leaves from the soup and serve over the cooked rice.
7. Serve hot and enjoy.

Spiced Coco Rice Noodles

Ingredients

- 8 oz. rice noodles
- cup bean sprouts
- 16 pcs. basil leaves, roughly chopped
- ¼ cup toasted coconut shreds
- 14oz. unsweetened coconut milk
- tbsp. tomato paste
- 1 tsp. chili powder
- pcs. green onions, sliced thin
- salt to taste

Directions

1. Cook the rice noodles according to packaging instructions. Set aside.
2. Heat the coconut milk in a pot over medium-high heat. Stir in the tomato paste, chili powder, and season with salt. Bring to a boil.
3. After boiling, reduce heat and allow to simmer for 3 minutes.
4. Combine the cooked rice noodles with the prepared sauce and top with the basil leaves, bean sprouts, and coconut shreds. Garnish with the sliced green onions.
5. Serve immediately and enjoy.

Baked Potato Bowl

Ingredients

- 4pcs. potatoes
- cup artichoke hearts in oil, quartered
- 1 tsp. olive oil
- ¼ cup olives, chopped
- 1 ½ tsp. lemon zest

Directions

1. Set oven at 400 F.
2. Clean the potatoes thoroughly and brush with the olive oil.
3. Place the potatoes on a baking sheet linked with parchment paper and bake for 1 hr. and 15 minutes.
4. While waiting for the potatoes, place the quartered artichokes in a bowl including the oil that came with it, the chopped olives, and lemon zest.
5. When the potatoes are tender divide in half and serve with the artichoke mixture on top.
6. Serve warm on a bowl and enjoy.

Hearty Squash Stew

Ingredients

- medium squash, peeled and sliced into chunks
- 16oz. cans black eyed peas, drained and rinsed
- tbsp. peanut oil
- 2 onions, diced
- cloves of garlic, chopped fine
- tbsp. ginger, grated
- 1 small green chili, chopped
- 1 tsp. cumin, ground
- tsp. salt
- cups low-sodium vegetable broth
- ½ cup peanut butter
- ½ cups tomato puree
- 2 tbsp. maple syrup
- 1 cup cooked brown rice
- 2 tbsp. roasted peanuts, chopped

Directions

1. Drizzle the peanut oil on a non-stick pan over medium heat. Throw in the onions and sauté for 15 minutes.
2. Throw in the grated ginger, green chili, chopped garlic, ground cumin, and salt. Stir and cook for 5 minutes.
3. Pour the vegetable broth, squash, peanut butter, the tomato puree, and maple syrup. Cook for 30 minutes or until the squash is tender.
4. Add the beans into the pot and stir. Allow to simmer for a few minutes.
5. Garnish with the chopped roast peanuts and serve hot with cooked rice on the side.

Red Peppers and Roast Almonds Penne

Ingredients

- ¾ lb. penne pasta
- 4 bell peppers, seeds removed and sliced into 4
- ½ cup roasted almonds, chopped
- ¾ cup olives
- ¼ cup olive oil
- tbsp. fresh thyme leaves
- salt and pepper to taste

Directions

1. Cook the pasta following the packing instructions (reserve ¼ of the pasta water).
2. Drain the pasta when cooked and return into the pot.
3. Preheat the broiler and lay the bell peppers on a baking sheet and place in the broiler for 8 minutes.
4. Remove the skin of the peppers and cut into 1-inch pieces and add into the pot with the pasta.
5. Add the remaining ingredients and toss them together.
6. Serve warm with slices of vegan bread on the side.

Eggplant Curry Rice Bowl

Ingredients

- cup long-grain rice
- large eggplant, cut into half-inch slices
- 15 oz. can chickpeas, drained and rinsed
- cups cherry tomatoes, cut in half
- ½ cup fresh basil leaves
- 1 onion, chopped
- 1 ½ tsp. curry powder
- salt and pepper to taste
- 1 tbsp. olive oil
- cups water

Directions

1. Cook the rice according to packaging instructions.
2. While waiting for the rice to cook, heat the oil in another saucepan over medium-high temperature. Throw in the onions and sauté for 5-6 minutes.
3. Add the eggplant, tomatoes, season with salt and pepper, and the curry powder. Stir and cook for 2 minutes.
4. Pour the water into the pan, cover, and bring to a boil.
5. After boiling reduce the heat and allow to simmer for 15 minutes.
6. Add the chickpeas to the pot and cook for another 3-4 minutes.
7. Turn off the heat and then add the basil leaves.
8. Serve the vegetables on top of the cooked rice in a bowl.

Homemade Hot Pot

Ingredients

- 4oz. thin rice noodles
- 8 oz. your favorite mushrooms, caps sliced thin
- 4 carrots, sliced thin
- 8 oz. green beans, cut into smaller pieces
- 6 cups low-sodium vegetable broth
- 2/3 cup tamari
- tbsp. ginger, grated
- pcs. green onions, sliced thin
- 1 tsp. Sriracha
- 1 tbsp. olive oil

Directions

1. Cook the noodles according to the packaging instructions.
2. While waiting for the noodles, pace a saucepan over medium fire. Drizzle with oil and throw in the mushroom slices. Cook and stir for 2 minutes.
3. Pour in the vegetable broth, tamari, grated ginger, and Sriracha and stir. Bring to a boil.
4. When boiling, add the green onions, sliced carrots, and green beans and simmer for 5 minutes or until the vegetable are cooked through.
5. Place the cooked noodles into serving bowls and ladle the broth on top of the noodles.
6. Serve hot.

Sweet and Spicy Tofu Chunks

Ingredients

- 7 oz. firm tofu
- tbsp. olive oil
- cups vegetables of your choice for stir-fry
- 1 clove of garlic, minced
- cups cooked brown rice.

For the sauce:

- 2 tbsp. Sriracha
- 3 tbsp. sweet chili sauce
- 2 tsps. low-sodium soy sauce

Directions

1. Prepare the tofu first by placing a paper towel on a plate and laying the firm tofu on it. Place another paper towel on top and add weight with another plate to extract the liquid form the tofu. Leave for an hour and allow the paper towels to absorb the liquid.
2. Slice the tofu into cubes.
3. Heat the olive oil on a pan over medium fire. When the oil is hot, throw in the tofu cubes and cook until they are golden brown on all sides. Set side.
4. Using the same pan, sauté the garlic first and then your choice of vegetables for stir-fry. Season with salt.
5. Meanwhile, whisk the ingredients of the sauce together in a small bowl.
6. Serve the cooked rice in a bowl topped with the cooked veggies and tofu and drizzle with the sauce.

Spinach Soup with Bowtie Pasta

Ingredients

- 4 cups spinach
- cup carrots, diced
- 1 cup celery, diced
- 1 onion, diced
- cloves of garlic, minced
- 6 cups vegetable broth
- 14 oz. can roasted diced tomatoes
- 8 oz. whole wheat pasta (vegan-friendly)
- ½ tsp. dried thyme
- ¼ tsp. dried rosemary
- ¼ tsp. dried oregano
- salt and pepper to taste
- tbsp. olive oil

Directions

1. Heat the olive oil on a large pot. Throw in the onions and sauté for 4 minutes.
2. Add the diced carrots, celery, and minced garlic into the pan and cook for 3-4 minutes.
3. Pour in the vegetable broth, canned tomatoes, and the pasta. Add in the herbs and then stir and bring to a boil.
4. Stir occasionally and reduce the heat. Allow to simmer for another 10 minutes or until the pasta is cooked.
5. Add the spinach leaves into the pot and cook for 2 minutes.
6. Season with salt and pepper and serve hot.

Homemade Vegan Pizza

Ingredients

- ½ store-bough garlic-herb pizza crust (make sure it's vegan friendly)
- pc. bell pepper, chopped
- 1 small onion, chopped
- 1 cup mushrooms, chopped
- ½ tsp. garlic powder
- ½ tsp. oregano
- ½ tsp. basil
- ¼ tsp. sea salt
- 1 tbsp. olive oil

For the sauce:

- 15 oz. can organic tomato sauce
- ½ tsp. garlic powder
- ½ tsp. oregano
- ½ tsp. basil
- ¼ tsp. sugar
- salt to taste

For the toppings:

- ½ cup vegan parmesan cheese
- (blitz cashews, salt, yeast, and garlic powder)
- red pepper flakes

Directions

1. Set the oven at 425F.
2. Heat a large pan over medium heat and drizzle with the olive oil. Sauté the onion and bell pepper and season with the herbs and salt. Stir and cook for 12-15 minutes.
3. Add the mushrooms right after 10 minutes of cooking. Set aside.
4. Prepare the sauce. In a mixing bowl, combine all the ingredients together. You can add water to achieve your preferred consistency. Set aside.
5. Roll the pizza dough and place on a baking sheet lined with parchment paper. Ladle the sauce on top and sprinkle with the vegan parmesan cheese and with the sautéed onions and bell pepper.
6. Place in the oven to cook on the middle rack for 20 minutes.
7. Serve while warm.

Peanut Sauce on Soba

Ingredients

- 8 oz. soba noodles, cooked according to package instructions
- cup mushrooms of your choice, sliced
- 1 pc. eggplant, chopped
- 1 red bell pepper, chopped
- pcs. green onion, chopped
- tsp. sesame seeds
- 2 tbsp. crushed peanuts
- 1 tsp. tamari
- 1 tbsp. olive oil

For the sauce:

- ¼ cup peanut butter
- tsp. tamari
- 1.5 tsp. lime juice
- 1/5 tbsp. sesame oil
- ½ tsp. ginger, grated
- 1 tsp. Sriracha
- water (if needed)

Directions

1. Prepare the sauce by whisking all the ingredients together in a bowl. Set aside.
2. Drizzle the olive oil in a pan and heat over medium temperature. Throw in the mushrooms, chopped eggplant and cook until the mushrooms are tender.
3. Add the red bell pepper in the pan along with the green onions and cook for 3-4 minutes.
4. Drizzle with tamari to add flavor. Turn off the heat.
5. Add the cooked rice noodles in the bowl with the peanut sauce and toss. Throw in the veggies and toss again.
6. Garnish with the crushed peanuts and sesame seeds.
7. Serve and enjoy.

Mushroom and Pepper Fajitas

Ingredients

- 2 jalapeno, seeded and sliced thin
- 2 red bell peppers, sliced
- cup Portobello mushrooms, stemmed and sliced thin
- 1 onion, cut into rounds
- ¼ tsp. garlic powder
- ¼ tsp. cumin
- ¼ tsp. sea salt
- 6 pcs. vegan tortilla wraps
- 1 tbsp. olive oil
- avocados, seeded and mashed
- ½ juice of lime
- 1 tsp. cilantro, chopped
- Sriracha sauce

Directions

1. Heat olive oil on a non-stick pan over medium-high temperature. Throw in the jalapeno, bell peppers, and onion. Season with the garlic powder, cumin, sea salt and sauté for a few minutes or until the onions soften. Transfer on a plate and set aside.
2. Using the same pan, throw in the mushrooms and season with salt. Cook until the mushroom is tender. Transfer to a dish, cover, and set aside.
3. Place the avocado meat in a bowl, cilantro, sprinkle with lime juice and mash to create a guacamole. Season with salt and pepper.
4. Warm the tortilla wraps and arrange the fajitas. Scoop the cooked mushrooms on the tortilla wraps, followed by the peppers, and guacamole on top.
5. Serve immediately and enjoy.

Roasted Sweet Potatoes

Ingredients

- 4 pcs. sweet potatoes
- 15 oz. chickpeas, drained and rinsed
- ½ tsp. cumin
- ½ tsp. cinnamon
- ½ tsp. coriander
- ½ tsp. paprika
- ¼ tsp. salt
- ½ tbsp. olive oil

For the sauce:

- ¼ cup hummus
- 3 cloves of garlic, minced
- tbsp. lemon juice
- tsp. fresh dill
- water (if needed)

For the toppings:

- 2 tbsp. lemon juice
- ¼ cup cherry tomatoes, chit in half
- ¼ cup fresh parsley, chopped
- tsp. chili garlic sauce

Directions

1. Set the oven at 400F.
2. Clean the sweet potatoes thoroughly and cut length wise.
3. In a baking sheet lined with foil, throw in the chickpeas and drizzle with oil. Add the spices and toss the ingredients together.
4. Brush the sweet potatoes with olive oil and add in the baking sheet with the chickpeas skin side up. Place in the oven to bake for 30-45 mins.
5. While waiting for the sweet potatoes to bake, prepare your sauce. Whisk all the ingredients together and add water if necessary if the sauce is too thick for your liking. Set aside.
6. Prepare the topping by tossing all the ingredients together in a bowl and then set aside to allow the tomatoes to marinate in the sauce.
7. Remove the tray from the oven when the sweet potatoes are tender.
8. Allow to cool for a bit before serving the potatoes.

9. To serve, flip the sweet potatoes and mash a little. Top with the baked chickpeas, drizzle with the prepared sauce, and garnish with the toppings.
10. Serve and consume immediately. Enjoy!

No-Sweat Brussels Sprouts Salad

Ingredients

- lb. brussels sprouts, grated on a food processor
- ½ cup almonds, silvered
- 1 green apple, peeled and cut in cubes

For the dressing:

- 2 tbsp. olive oil (divided in 2)
- tbsp. mustard
- tbsp. lime juice

Directions

1. Place the silvered almonds in a heated pan and toast until they are light brown.
2. Remove the almonds and drizzle the 1 tbsp. olive oil into the pan and place over medium heat. Throw in the grated brussels sprouts and cook for 3-4 minutes.
3. Prepare the dressing by whisking all the ingredients in a bowl.
4. Toss the cooked brussles sprouts, apples, toasted almonds, and drizzle dressing on top. Toss and serve immediately.

Thai Salad with Peanut Sauce

Ingredients

- ¼ cup tofu, cut in cubes
- 3 tsp. low-sodium soy sauce
- cup red cabbage, shredded
- pcs. radishes, sliced thin
- ½ cucumber, julienne
- ½ carrot, shredded
- ¼ red bell pepper, sliced thin
- 1 green onion, chopped
- ¼ cup fresh cilantro, chopped
- tbsp. peanuts, roasted

For the dressing:

- ½ tsp. chili garlic sauce
- ½ pc. ginger
- 2 tbsp. rice wine vinegar
- 2 tbsp. peanut butter
- tbsp. low-sodium soy sauce
- 1 clove of garlic
- 1 tbsp. water
- ½ tsp. sesame oil
- ½ lime, cut into wedges

Directions

1. Marinate the tofu cubes into the low-sodium soy sauce for not less than 15 minutes.
2. Heat a non-stick pan drizzled with olive oil over medium-high fire and fry the tofu for 3-4 minutes on each side or until they are crispy. Set aside.
3. Prepare the dressing by whisking all the ingredients (except the lime wedges) in a bowl and set aside.
4. Layer all the sliced vegetables on a bowl, top with the cooked tofu and garnish with the green onions, cilantro, and peanuts. Serve with the prepared sauce and lime wedges on the side.
5. Serve immediately and enjoy.

Vegan Burgers

Ingredients

- ¾ lentils
- ¾ cups gluten-free/vegan bread crumbs
- ¼ brown rice, cooked
- ½ onion, chopped
- 2 cloves of garlic
- 5 pcs. pickled beets
- white miso paste
- tbsp. peanut butter
- tbsp. yeast
- ¼ tsp. thyme
- ¼ tsp. sage
- ¼ tsp. chili powder
- ¼ tsp. mustard powder
- ground pepper to taste

Directions

1. Place the pickled beets in a food processor and pulse until the beets are well chopped.
2. Add all the ingredients to the food processor. Don't forget to scrape the sides to combine all the ingredients in the blender. Make sure that your patty doesn't turn into a messy mush, so don't over-pulse.
3. Transfer the patty mixture into a container and chill in the fridge 40-60 minutes.
4. When the mixture it firm enough, form them with your hands into burger patties.
5. Grease a non-stick pan with olive oil or cooking spray and place over medium heat.
6. Cook each side of the patty for 10 minutes each or more or until the outer layer is crispy.
7. Serve with vegan buns or just with crispy lettuce.

Vegan-Friendly Pho

Ingredients

- onion, quartered
- 4 cloves of garlic, chopped
- whole cloves
- star anise
- pc. cinnamon stick
- 1 tsp. ginger, sliced
- 10 cups vegetable broth
- low-sodium soy to taste
- 1 package rice noodles, cooked according to instructions

For the toppings

- ½ bean sprouts
- bunch fresh Thai basil
- pcs. green onions, chopped
- ¼ cup cilantro leaves, roughly chopped
- ¼ cup mint leaves, roughly chopped
- lemon wedges
- Sriracha (optional)

Directions

1. Pour the vegetable broth in a pot and add the onion, garlic, cloves, star anise, cinnamon, and ginger. Cover and simmer for 30 minutes.
2. Add 2 tbsp. of soy if needed.
3. Place the cooked rice noodles in serving bowls, top with the prepared toppings and ladle over the vegetable stock.
4. Serve with lemon wedges on the top or with Sriracha.
5. Enjoy hot!

Classic Tomato and Basil Pasta

Ingredients

- 3 large ripe tomatoes
- ½ cup basil leaves
- ¼ tsp. chili flakes
- ½ onion, chopped
- clove of garlic, chopped
- ¼ tsp. salt
- cups gluten-free pasta, cooked according to packaging
- vegan parmesan cheese

Directions

1. Prepare the sauce while cooking the pasta. Place the tomatoes, basil, onion, and garlic in a bowl. Sprinkle with chili flakes and season with salt. Toss and allow to sit for 10 minutes or until the pasta is cooked.
2. Drain the pasta from the pot and set aside. Using the same pot (while it is hot), throw in the prepared tomatoes and basil. Stir and add the pasta back into the pan.
3. Toss the ingredients together and sprinkle with vegan parmesan on top.

Quick-Cook Coco-Curry

Ingredients

For the quinoa:

- cup quinoa
- 2 ½ cups light coconut milk
- ½ cup water
- tbsp. agave nectar

For the curry sauce:

- 1 tbsp. curry powder
- ¼ tsp. cayenne pepper
- 2 14 oz. light coconut milk
- 1 cup vegetable broth
- ½ cup broccoli florets
- ¼ cup tomatoes, diced
- ¼ cup snow peas, cut
- ½ cup carrots, diced
- 4 cloves of garlic, minced
- 1 onion, diced
- 1 tbsp. ginger, grated
- salt and pepper to taste
- 1 tbsp. olive oil

Directions

1. Wash the quinoa thoroughly. Throw the quinoa in a saucepan and heat for 3 minutes. Pour in the coconut milk and water. Stir and bring to a boil.
2. When boiling, reduce heat, cover, and allow to simmer for 15 minutes or until the quinoa is cooked through and fluffy.
3. While waiting for the quinoa to cook, heat another sauce pan over medium temperature and drizzle the 1 tbsp. olive oil.
4. Sauté the minced garlic, onions, and ginger for 2-3 minutes and then add the broccoli, carrots, and season with salt and pepper. Stir frequently and cook for 5-8 minutes.
5. Add the curry powder with the vegetables, along with the cayenne pepper. Pour in the coconut milk and vegetable broth. Season with salt and stir well.
6. Bring to a simmer and cook for 10 minutes.
7. And then add the snow peas and add the tomatoes and cook for another 5 minutes.
8. Place the cooked quinoa on a serving bowl and serve with the curried vegetables on top.

Philly Cheese Steak

Ingredients

- 1 cup seitan, cut into strips
- 1 onion, sliced
- 1 bell pepper, sliced thin
- ¼ tsp. ground black pepper
- ¼ tsp. cayenne powder
- salt to taste
- 1 tbsp. olive oil
- 5 tbsp. vegan cheddar cheese
- fresh cilantro, chopped tomatoes, and chopped jalapenos for garnish
- 2 vegan sub sandwich cut in half

Directions

1. Lightly brush the subs with olive oil and toast the subs in the oven.
2. Heat the olive oil in a non-stick pan over medium heat, and then add the bell pepper, onion, and season with salt. Cook for a few minutes or until the onions begin to caramelize.
3. Add the vegan cheddar cheese on top of the cooking vegetables and transfer into a plate. Set aside.
4. Using the same pan (while it's still hot) add another 1 tbsp. of olive oil and cook the seitan strips. Turn of the kit and set aside
5. Scoop the cooked veggies on top of the warm subs and then followed by the seitan and your garnishes.
6. Serve immediately and enjoy.

Roasted Vegetable Salad

Ingredients

- 1 head of garlic, end cut off
- 1 bunch beets, washed thoroughly
- 1 bunch beet greens, rinsed
- 1 bunch carrots, washed thoroughly and peeled
- ½ juice of lemon
- 2 tbsp. extra virgin olive oil
- 3 tbsp. olive oil
- 1/3 cup hulled pepitas, toasted
- salt and pepper to taste

Directions

1. Set the oven at 350F.
2. Pour water on a pot and bring to a boil on the stove.
3. Meanwhile, place the head of garlic on top of a foil, drizzle with oil and season with salt. Wrap the garlic with the foil and place on a baking tray and cook in oven for 15 minutes.
4. After 15 minutes, remove the garlic from the oven, set aside, and allow to cool.
5. Adjust the oven temperature to 425F.
6. Place the carrots in the boiling water and blanch for 2 minutes. Set aside.
7. Add the beets into the boiling water and cook for 8 minutes. Remove the beets and then run on tap water. Remove the skins from the beets.
8. Cut the carrots in half and quarter the beets.
9. Place the veggies on two separate baking dishes and drizzle with the olive oil and season with salt.
10. Transfer in the oven and roast for at least 15 minutes. Don't forget to flip the vegetables halfway through cooking.
11. Place the beet greens on a baking sheet and brush the leave with the olive oil. Season again with salt and place in the oven to bake for 5 minutes or until the leaves has softened.
12. Prepare the dressing while waiting for the veggies. Remove the skin from the roasted garlic and place in a bowl. Mash the garlic and add the juice of lemon and season with salt. Add the extra virgin olive oil and whisk until the dressing has emulsified.
13. Place all the roasted carrots and beets in a bowl and drizzle with the dressing. Toss and then serve on a bowl layered with the roasted beet greens. Garnish with toasted pepitas on top. Season again with salt and pepper.

Hot Chickpea Sliders

Ingredients

- 15 oz. chickpeas, drained and rinsed
- 1 cup quick cook oats
- ½ onion, chopped
- 3 tbsp. cilantro leaves, chopped
- 1 zucchini grated
- 2 tbsp. wine vinegar
- 2 tbsp. peanut butter
- 1 tsp. garlic powder
- 1 tsp. cumin
- 2 tsp. black pepper, ground
- salt to taste
- 1 tbsp. Sriracha
- 2 tbsp. olive oil

Directions

1. Mash the chickpeas in a bowl using a fork.
2. Add all the ingredients in the bowl and mix well using your hands.
3. For the mixture into small patties.
4. Place on a grill set for about 400F and cook for 10 minutes on each side.
5. Serve with small vegan burger buns.
6. Add with your favorite toppings such as shredded cabbage, onions, and more hot sauce.

__Crispy Steak:__

Ingredients
- 1 block firm tofu, cut into steak-sized pieces
- 2 tbsp. tomato paste
- 1 tbsp. mustard
- 1 tbsp. low-sodium soy sauce
- 1 tbsp. maple syrup
- 4 cloves of garlic, minced
- ½ tsp. pepper, ground
- ½ vegan breadcrumbs
- 1 tbsp. water
- 2 tbsp. olive oil
- vegan-friendly barbecue sauce for dip

Directions
1. Drain the tofu and place on a dish towel. Wrap with paper towel and place weight on top to squeeze out excess liquid. Allow to sit for 20-30 minutes.
2. Place the minced garlic in a large bowl and add all the remaining ingredients into the bowl. Combine well.
3. Coat the tofu steaks into the mixture making sure to cover every side.
4. Heat the 2 tbsp. olive oil (or more) on a non-stick pan over medium temperature. Cook the steaks for 4-5 minutes on each side, or until they turn golden brown. Careful when handling tofu; best use a large spatula to cook.
5. Serve the steaks warm with the dipping sauce on the side.

<u>Desserts</u>

Creamy Chocolate Mousse

Ingredients
- 1 large ripe banana
- 4 dates
- ½ avocado
- 2 tbsp. shredded coconut, unsweetened
- 3 tbsp. cacao powder
- 1 tsp vanilla extract
- 1 tsp pure maple syrup
- 1 dash, almond milk

Toppings:
- Mixed berries
- Cacao nibs
- Coarsely chopped nuts

Directions
1. Combine all the ingredients apart from the almond milk and cacao powder in a blender and pulse until creamy and smooth.
2. Serve into bowls and fold in the cacao powder, add the dash of milk. Chill in the fridge for about 2 hours then add your toppings and enjoy!

Fruity Kebabs Dusted With Cacao Powder

Ingredients

- 3 pineapple slices
- 2 mandarins
- 1 apple
- Add any fruit of choice
- 2 tbsp. cacao powder

Directions

Cut the fruit into bite sized portions and stick on skewers or tooth picks to make mini kebabs. Dust with cacao powder and pop in the fridge to chill for 1 hour. Enjoy!

Chewy Peanut Butter Bites

Ingredients

- ½ cup peanut butter, natural
- 1/3 cup rolled oats
- ¼ cup quick oats
- ¼ cup coconut flakes, unsweetened
- ¼ cup brown rice crisp cereal
- ¼ cup apple cider
- ¼ cup wheat germ
- 1 tbsp. pure maple syrup
- ½ tsp cinnamon

Directions

1. Mix all the ingredients in a large bowl except the cereal and combine well until evenly blended.
2. Mold the mixture into 16 medium sized balls.
3. Pour the brown rice cereal into a large tray or shallow bowl and roll each of the balls until coated on all sides.
4. Chill in the fridge for 2-4 hours or overnight for better results. Enjoy!

Indian Chai Pancakes

Serving size: Makes 4 large pancakes

Ingredients

- 2/3 cup whole-wheat pastry flour
- 1/4 teaspoon salt
- 2 teaspoons baking powder
- 2/3 cup almond milk
- 1/4 teaspoon freshly ground black pepper
- 1/4 teaspoon ground cloves
- 1/4 teaspoon ground cardamom
- 1 teaspoon ground cinnamon
- 2 teaspoons freshly grated ginger
- Non-stick cooking spray (optional if using a non-stick pan)

Directions

1. Mix the flour, salt, baking powder, pepper, cloves, cardamom, cinnamon, and ginger together in a metal bowl.
2. Add the almond to the dry ingredients and mix them until they are well combined.
3. Put this mixture in a measuring cup.
4. Using a non-stick) on medium heat, pour 1/3 cup pancake batter onto the middle of the pan.
5. When the top side bubbles and is mostly firm, flip the pancake over.
6. Keep this on the heat for another 1 to 1½ minutes.
7. Repeat until you've used all the batter.

Protein Rich Stuffed Strawberries

Ingredients

- 24 strawberries
- 1 ripe banana
- ¼ cup quinoa, uncooked
- 12 almonds, chopped
- ½ tsp cinnamon
- ½ tsp almond extract
- 1 tsp cocoa powder, unsweetened
- ½ tbsp. pure maple syrup

Directions

1. Add the quinoa and one cup of water to a medium pot and place over medium flame. Bring to a boil then lower the flame and simmer for 15 minutes, until the quinoa is fluffy and light.
2. Now combine the cooked quinoa, banana, cocoa powder, cinnamon, maple syrup, and almond extract in a large bowl and mix well then set aside for it cool.
3. Clean the berries and gently pat them dry. Use a paring knife, preferably a small one, to remove the tops and to also scoop out some of the flesh of each berry.
4. You can combine the scooped out flesh with the quinoa mixture if so desired then scoop this mixture into the center of each berry. Finally top with the almonds and chill in the fridge for an hour or two before serving. Enjoy!

Vegan Brownies To-Die For

Ingredients

- 2 cups vegan chocolate chips
- ½ cup cocoa powder, unsweetened
- ½ cup apple sauce, unsweetened
- ¾ cups and 2 tbsp. chickpea flour
- 2 tbsp. arrowroot
- 2 ¼ baking powder
- ¼ baking soda
- ¼ tsp. xanthan gum
- ¼ cup potato starch
- 1 tsp. salt
- 10 ½ tbsp. agave nectar
- 2 tbsp. vanilla
- ½ cup black coffee, brewed
- ½ cup olive oil

Directions

1. Set the oven at 325F
2. In a bowl, combine the chickpea flour, arrowroot, baking powder, baking soda, xanthan gum, potato starch, salt, agave nectar, and cocoa powder. Mix well.
3. In another bowl, combine the apple sauce, olive oil, and vanilla extract. Gradually add the dry ingredients into this bowl. Stir well.
4. Add the coffee followed by the vegan chocolate chips and stir.
5. Brush small muffin pans with oil and then scoop 1 tbsp. of batter into the muffin pan and repeat until you've finished all the batter.
6. Place in the oven to bake for 12 minutes or more or until the toothpick comes out clean after inserting into the brownie.
7. Remove from the oven and allow to cool for 15 minutes before removing from the pan and serving.

Refreshing Watermelon Bowl

Ingredients

- 6 lbs. watermelon, cut into chunks and chilled
- 2 tbsp. mint leaves, chopped
- 2 tbsp. lime juice
- 2 tbsp. light rum
- 2 tbsp. brown sugar
- ¼ tsp. salt

Directions

1. In a salad bowl, combine the lime juice, rum, sugar, and salt. Whisk well.
2. Add the watermelon in the bowl, add the chopped mint leaves, and chop well.
3. Serve immediately on a bowl or store in the fridge to chill for up to 2 hours.

Frozen Banana Pops

Ingredients

- 3 ripe bananas, cut into smaller pieces
- ½ cup orange juice
- ½ cup lemon juice
- 8 oz. crushed pineapples
- mint leaves, chopped (for garnish)
- ½ cup sugar
- 1 ½ cup water

Directions

1. Place the sugar and the water in a sauce pan. Stir and bring into a bowl. Turn off the heat and allow to cool.
2. Pour the syrup in a dish and add the remaining ingredients. Pour the mixture into popsicle molds.
3. Place in the freezer for up to 3 hours or until the popsicles are totally frozen.

Peaches and Berries

Ingredients

- 2 cups water
- 1 ¼ cups sugar
- 1 small cinnamon stick
- ¾ dry white wine
- ½ tsp. lemon zest
- 1 tbsp. lemon juice
- 6 peaches, pitted and cut in half
- 1 cup raspberries

Directions

1. In a pot combine all the first five ingredients and bring into a bowl. Add the halved peaches in the pot and cover with parchment paper to make sure the peaches are submerged in the liquid.
2. Lower the heat and allow to simmer for 8 minutes more.
3. Turn of the heat and stir in the lemon juice. Add ½ cup of the raspberries, cover again with the parchment paper, and allow to cool. Allow to sit for 30 minutes before transferring into the fridge to chill for not less than 2 hours.
4. Remove the peaches from the pot and remove the skin.
5. Use a strainer to discard the solids in the syrup.
6. Serve the chilled peaches with the remaining ½ raspberries on top.

Tropical Zest

Ingredients

- 2 pcs. limes, juiced
- zest from the two limes
- ¼ cup sugar
- a pinch of salt
- 1 pc. apple, sliced thin
- 1 mango, pitted and sliced thin
- 1 papaya, seeded, peeled and sliced thin

Directions

1. Place the lime zest, 2 tsp. lime juice, sugar, and salt in a food processor and pulse.
2. Place the apples on a bowl, pour over the remaining lime juice, and toss. Add the sliced mango and papaya with the apples and sprinkle with the prepared sugar.
3. Serve immediately and enjoy!

Warm Papaya

Ingredients

- 2 tbsp. brown sugar
- ¼ tsp. ginger, ground
- 2 medium-sized papayas, cut in half and seeds removed
- ¼ tsp. cayenne pepper
- 1 pc. lime, cut into wedges

Directions

1. Set oven at 450F.
2. In a bowl mix the brown sugar and ginger.
3. Lay the papayas on a baking sheet and generously sprinkle with the sugar and ginger mixture.
4. Place the papayas in the oven to roast for 35 minutes. Remember to brush with the caramel (melted sugar) once in a while, while roasting.
5. Add a dash of cayenne before serving. Enjoy warm!

Choco-Pear Indulgence

Ingredients

- 4oz. 70% cacao (vegan dark chocolate), chopped
- 4 pears, pitted

Directions

1. Melt the dark chocolate on a double boiler and stir until smooth. Allow to cool for a few minutes.
2. Dip the pear into the melted chocolate covering ¾ of the fruit.
3. Transfer the coated pears on a baking sheet lined with parchment paper and place in the fridge to allow the chocolate to set for not less than 15 minutes.
4. Serve on room temperature. Enjoy!

Cinnamon Apple Roast

Ingredients

- 1/4 cup sugar
- 1/8 tsp. cinnamon
- 6 pcs. apples, core removed and cut into 4

Directions

1. Set oven at 400F.
2. In a bowl mix the sugar and cinnamon. Toss the apple slices in the bowl and toss to cover with the sugar.
3. Place the coated apple on a baking sheet lined with parchment paper, making sure that the apples are spread in a single later.
4. Cook in the oven for 30 minutes. Toss the apples on the 15 minute mark.
5. Allow the apples to cool down for a few minutes before serving.

Chewy Almond Balls

Ingredients

- 1/4 cup almond butter
- 3 tbsp. brown rice syrup
- 1 tsp. vanilla
- 1 tbsp. chocolate chips
- 1 cup rice crisps

Directions

1. Combine the almond butter, vanilla, and syrup on a bowl and place in the microwave on high for 40 seconds.
2. Stir the syrup and add the rice crisps with the chocolate cups. Stir until all the ingredients are well incorporated.
3. Wet your hands first before forming the mixture into small balls.
4. Place the balls on a plate covered with parchment paper and place in the freezer to set for at least 5 minutes.
5. Enjoy.

Medjool Dates Squares

Ingredients

- 10 dates, pitted and chopped
- 1 ½ cups whole almonds
- 1 ½ cups oats
- ¼ cup coconut oil, melted
- ½ tsp. salt

For the filling:

- 25 pcs. dates, pitted and chopped
- ½ cup water

Directions

1. Place the almonds and oats in a food processors and pulse until the ingredients are crumbled.
2. Add the dates and then pulse again until the dates are crumbly.
3. Pour the coconut oil in the food processor and continue blending until the mixture turns sticky.
4. Set aside ¾ cup of the mixture and then transfer the remaining into a square baking pan lined with 2 layers of parchment paper. Spread evenly.
5. Place the ingredients for the filling in the food processor and blend until it turns into a paste.
6. Scoop the filling and spread over the mixture on the pan.
7. Cover with the remaining ¾ cup dates mixture.
8. Place in the fridge to chill for 1-2 hours. Cut into bite-sized squares and serve.

Homemade Melon Popsicles

Ingredients

- 1 1/3 cups honeydew, seeded and cut into chunks
- 1 tbsp. fresh orange juice
- 1 1/3 cup cantaloupe, cut into chunks.
- 1 tbsp. limeade concentrate

Directions

1. Place the melon in a blender and add the orange juice. Blend until smooth
2. Pour the mixture into popsicle molds and place in the freezer for at least 30 minutes.
3. Blend the cantaloupe with the limeade concentrate and then pour over the honeydew mixture on the popsicle molds.
4. Freeze again for at least 3 hours before serving. s

Zesty Pear Popsicles

Ingredients

- 15 oz. pear halves
- ¼ cup limeade concentrate
- 2 tsp. lime zest, grated

Directions

1. Drain the syrup from the pear, but reserve ¼ cup for the syrup.
2. Place the syrup, pears, and the rest of the ingredients in a blender and blend until smooth.
3. Pour the mixture into popsicle molds and freeze for up to 1.5 hours.

Quick Herbed Pear Slices

Ingredients

- 3 pcs. pears
- ¼ cup orange juice
- 1 tbsp. rosemary, chopped
- ¼ cup sugar

Directions

1. Remove the core from the pear and cut into thick slices.
2. Place the pears on a serving plate and sprinkle with the orange juice.
3. Toss and then sprinkle with the chopped rosemary and sugar.
4. Serve and enjoy.

Homemade PB and Choco Chip Ice Cream

Ingredients

- 2 frozen ripe bananas
- 2 tbsp. all-natural peanut butter
- 3 tbsp. raw cacao nibs
- 1/8 tsp. sea salt
- 1 tsp. maple syrup

Directions

1. Place the frozen banana in a food processor and blend until crumbly.
2. Add the rest of the ingredients and process until you achieve a consistency that looks like a soft-serve ice cream.
3. Drizzle with maple syrup on top before serving.

Protein-Packed Dessert Balls

Ingredients

- 12 pcs. Medjool dates, pitted
- ¼ cup chia seeds
- ¼ cup hemp seeds, hulled
- ¼ cup sesame seeds
- ¼ cup dark chocolate chips
- ¼ cup cocoa powder
- ¼ tsp. cinnamon
- 1/8 tsp. sea salt
- ½ tsp. vanilla

Directions

1. Place the dates in a food processor and pulse until it turns into a paste-like consistency.
2. Add the rest of the ingredients except the chocolate chips and pulse until all the ingredients are well combined.
3. Add the chips last and pulse for a few times.
4. Form the mixture into small balls using your hands.
5. Place the balls on a plate or container and freeze for at least 20 minutes.
6. Enjoy.

Gluten-Free Choco Macaroons

Ingredients

- 1 pc. ripe banana, mashed
- ¼ cup agave nectar
- ½ tsp. vanilla
- ¼ cup melted coconut oil
- 6 tbsp. cocoa powder
- 1 ½ coconut shreds
- 1 tbsp. chia seeds
- 1/8 tsp. sea sat

Directions

1. Place the mashed bananas in a bowl and add the coconut oil, agave nectar, coconut oil, and vanilla. Mix well.
2. Add the sifted coconut powder to the mixture and stir well.
3. Add the coconut shreds and chia seeds with the sea salt and mix again.
4. Line a baking tray with parchment paper and scoop the macaroons mixture using a small ice cream scooper on the tray.
5. Place in the freezer to set for not less than 20 minutes.
6. Enjoy!

Strawberries in Syrup

Ingredients

- 1 lb. strawberries, cut in half
- 1 cup sugar
- 1 cup water
- ¼ tsp. vanilla
- ½ tsp. lime zest

Directions

1. Pour the water in a sauce pan and stir in the sugar. Heat the pan over medium temperature. Add the vanilla and lime zest and allow to simmer for a minute.
2. Place the strawberry halves on a serving bowl and pour over the hot syrup.
3. Allow to cool to room temperature before serving.

Choco Banana Pops

Ingredients

- 1 cup semi-sweet chocolate
- 2 pcs. ripe banana, cut in half
- ½ cup peanuts, roughly chopped

Directions

1. Melt the chocolate on a double boiler and stir.
2. Stick popsicles on the banana halves and dip onto the melted chocolate. Make sure that the banana is well coated.
3. Sprinkle with the peanuts and place on a baking sheet lined with parchment paper.
4. Place in the fridge to chill for not less than 30 minutes.
5. Enjoy.

Peanut Butter Bites

Ingredients

- ¼ cup all-natural peanut butter
- 2 tbsp. coconut oil, melted
- ¼ tsp. vanilla
- 2 tbsp. maple syrup
- ¼ salt

Directions

1. Place all the ingredients in a bowl and stir well, making sure the ingredients are mixed together.
2. Pour the mixture onto a container lined with parchment paper.
3. Place in the freezer to set firm for not less than 40 minutes.
4. Remove from the freezer and allow to sit for 5 minutes before cutting into bite-sized squares.
5. Enjoy.

Coco-Mango Pudding

Ingredients

- ½ cup almond milk
- ½ cup coconut milk
- 1 tbsp. coconut shreds
- 1 fresh mango, chopped
- 2 tbsp. chia seeds
- agave nectar for drizzle
- 1 tsp. lime zest

Directions

1. Combine the milks in a jar with a lid and shake.
2. Add the chia seeds to the jar and the coconut shreds. Stir well.
3. Then add the mango and place in the fridge.
4. And then drizzle the agave nectar and place in the freezer to chill for 6 hours.
5. Shake the jar again and then transfer into the fridge for another 24 hours.
6. Garnish with lime zest before serving.

Homemade Hemp Protein Ice Cream

Ingredients

- 1/3 cup almond milk
- 2 ripe bananas, frozen and sliced
- ¼ hemp powder, vanilla flavor
- 1 tsp. vanilla
- 1 cup baby spinach
- 1 tbsp. almond butter

Directions

1. Throw all the ingredients in a blender and blend until you achieve a consistency of a soft-serve ice cream.
2. Serve immediately and enjoy.

Chocolate Coated Apple Crips

Ingredients

- 1 pc apple
- ¼ cup roasted almonds, chopped
- 2 tbsp. vegan chocolate chips, chopped
- ¼ tsp. vanilla
- 4 tbsp. organic granulated sugar
- 2 ½ coconut cream
- 1/8 tsp. salt

Directions

1. Pierce the apple on top with a wooden stick.
2. In a dish mix the chopped nuts and chocolate chips and set aside.
3. Place a pan over medium-high heat and then stir together the granulated sugar, coconut cream, vanilla, and salt. Stir until bubbles starts to appear.
4. Simmer for 45 seconds. Reduce the heat to low and allow to simmer for another minute.
5. Transfer the mixture into dish and place in the fridge until the mixture becomes sticky.
6. Roll the apple on the syrup and then roll again on the chopped nuts and choco chips.
7. Serve and enjoy!

Acai Fruit Bowl

Ingredients

- 1 pack acai puree, unsweetened
- 1 ripe banana
- ½ cup blueberries
- ½ cup raspberries
- ½ cup almond milk
- your preferred toppings (ex. granola, coconut shreds, chia seeds, nuts, etc.)

Directions

1. Place the acai and banana into a blender and blend until smooth.
2. Arrange your berries and preferred toppings on a bowl and pour over the acai mixture.
3. Serve immediately and enjoy.

Cherries Dipped in Chocolate

Ingredients

- 12 pcs. cherries, pitted (make sure that the stems are intact)
- ½ cup vegan chocolate chips

Directions

1. Wash the cherries and place on a baking tray lined with parchment paper.
2. Melt the chocolate on a double boiler and stir.
3. Dip the cherries in the chocolate and place back on the baking tray.
4. Place in the fridge to set for about an hour before serving.

Vegan Peach Pies

Ingredients

- 8 pcs. peaches, pitted, peeled and sliced
- 3 tbsp. whole-wheat flour
- 1 cup organic brown sugar
- ¼ tsp. cinnamon
- 1 tbsp. lemon juice
- 2 store-bought vegan pie crusts

Directions

1. Set oven at 350F
2. Place the peaches in a bowl and sprinkle with the flour, sugar, and cinnamon. Drizzle with lemon juice and toss. Let it rest for 10 minutes.
3. Transfer the filling onto the pie crust and top the pie with the second pie crust.
4. Poke small holes on the top of the pie before baking in the oven for 35-40 minutes.
5. Serve warm.

Smoothie Recipes

Decadent Lime Tart Smoothie

Ingredients

- 4 tbsp lime juice
- ½ avocado
- 2 cups of swiss chard
- 1 large frozen banana
- 2 cups coconut milk
- ¼ cup cashews (soaked if you do not have a high power blender to pulverize)
- 2 tbsp coconut butter
- 2 tbsp chia seed
- ½ tsp vanilla extract (optional)
- Zest of 1 lime (to taste)
- stevia to taste

Directions:

1. Place all ingredients into a blender
2. Blend on high until smooth
3. Serve and enjoy

Minty Choc Chip Smoothie

Ingredients

- 1/2 cup almond milk
- 2 cups spinach
- 1 medium frozen banana
- 2 tbsp shelled hemp seeds
- 6 ice cubes
- 1/2 cup boiling water
- 1 peppermint tea bag
- 3 tbsp raw cacao nibs

Directions:

1. Steep the tea in the 1/2 cup boiling water for about 30 minutes
2. Wait until the water has cooled, about 30 minutes. (to make this process easier make the tea at night and let it sit overnight.
3. Place all ingredients but cacao nibs in the blender.
4. Blend until smooth.
5. Drop in half of the cacao nibs and pulse quickly.
6. Top with leftover nibs.

Apple Pie Smoothie

Ingredients

- 1/2 tsp cinnamon
- 1/2 tsp nutmeg
- 1 tbsp almond butter
- 1/2 cup unsweetened coconut milk
- 1 small apple, sliced
- 1/2 cup rolled oats
- 3-4 ice cubes
- 1/2 cup cold water

Directions

1. Add oats and water into the blender. Pulse and allow the mixture to sit for at least 2-3 minutes so the oats can soften.
2. Add all the remaining ingredients to the blender. Process until smooth, about 30 seconds. Pour into a glass and sprinkle with a little extra cinnamon and nutmeg.
3. Enjoy!

Creamy Kale & Avo Smoothie Bowl

Ingredients

- ½ cup raspberries
- 1 kiwi, sliced
- 1 tsp chia seeds
- 1 cup kale leaves
- 1 cup almond milk
- 1 banana, sliced
- ½ avocado
- ½ cup ice
- 1 Tbsp. agave syrup, plus additional for serving

Directions

1. Blend the kale, almond milk, ½ of the banana, avocado, ice, and 1 tablespoon of the agave until smooth.
2. Transfer to a bowl and top with the raspberries, kiwi, chia seeds, remaining ½ banana, and a drizzle of agave.

Buckwheat & Blueberry Smoothie Bowl

Ingredients

- 1/2 cup almond milk or water
- 1 banana
- juice of half a lemon
- 1 teaspoon vanilla
- 1 cup buckwheat groats, soaked overnight
- 2 cups blueberries
- 2 tablespoons maple syrup

Directions

1. Submerge buckwheat in water and let sit overnight. Drain and rinse well the next morning.
2. In a blender or food processor, blend the blueberries with maple syrup until smooth.
3. Add buckwheat, milk or water, banana, lemon juice and vanilla to the remaining blueberry puree and blend until smooth.
4. Serve the buckwheat porridge.

Tropical Mango and Pineapple Smoothie Bowl

Ingredients
- ¾ cup frozen mango
- ¾ cup frozen pineapple
- 1 small banana
- ½ cup coconut water
- ¼ fresh mango
- 1 sliced kiwi
- 2 dates, torn
- 2 Tbsp. shredded coconut

Directions
1. Place all ingredients into a blender
2. Blend on high until smooth
3. Transfer to a bowl and top with the fresh mango, kiwi, dates, and coconut.

Lemon Poppy Smoothie

Ingredients

- 1 1/2 cup rice milk
- 1/2 cup raspberries
- 2 tbsp rolled oats
- 1 tbsp lemon juice
- 1 tbsp almond butter
- 1 tbsp chia seeds
- 1 1/2 tsp poppy seeds
- 1 tsp pure vanilla extract
- zest from 1 small lemon
- pinch stevia powder

Toppings

- raspberries + lemon

Directions

1. To be made the night before or 4 hours in advance.
2. Combine all ingredients in a mason jar/glass container and place in the fridge overnight.
3. In the morning, pour ingredients into blender and process until smooth.

Matcha Mint Dream

Ingredients

- 1/3 cup soaked raw cashews
- 3 cups swiss chard
- 3 frozen bananas
- 1/4 cup mint leaves
- 1 1/2 tsp vanilla extract or vanilla powder
- 2 tsp matcha powder
- 3 tbsp hemp seeds
- 3 1/2 cups unsweetened almond milk
- maple syrup or stevia to taste
- 1 tbsp cacao nibs

Directions

1. In blender, combine all ingredients except for the cacao nibs
2. Blend on high until totally smooth.
3. Add the cacao nibs into the blender and pulse once or twice
4. Pour into a glass or bowl and enjoy

Mango, Chia & Blueberry Smoothie

Ingredients
- 100g unsalted cashew nuts
- 300ml chilled water
- 1 ripe mango, stoned and flesh chopped
- 1 cup blueberries
- 1/4 cup ice cubes
- 1 tablespoon linseeds or chia seeds
- 1 tablespoon porridge oats
- 1 tablespoon honey

Directions
1. Soak cashew nuts in plenty of water overnight.
2. Drain the water in the morning.
3. Blend the cashews in the blender along with 100ml chilled water.
4. Form a thick paste, then add 200ml chilled water and process until you get smooth creamy cashew milk.
5. Add all the other ingredients and blend until smooth.
6. Pour in tall glasses and garnish with mango cubes and blueberries.

Almond Honeydew Smoothie

Ingredients

- 2 cups honeydew, diced (this was half of a melon for me)
- 2 cups, organic unsweetened almond milk
- 1-2 cups of ice

Directions

1. Place all ingredients into a blender
2. Blend on high until smooth
3. Serve and enjoy

<u>Get Your Vitamin C Smoothie</u>

Ingredients

- 2 bananas
- 1 orange
- 2 kiwis
- 10-12 frozen strawberries
- ½ cup of frozen blueberries
- 1-2 cups of orange juice

Directions

1. Place all ingredients into a blender
2. Blend on high until smooth
3. Serve and enjoy

Kale Citrus Smoothie

Ingredients

- 1.5 cups kale
- 1 medium apple
- 1 cup orange juice
- 1 banana
- 1 tsp minced ginger root
- ½ tsp ground cinnamon
- 1 tbsp chia or flax seeds

Directions

1. Add banana, apple and kale with stems removed into your blender. Mince your fresh ginger and add to jug.
2. Blend until smooth.
3. Serve immediately

Coconut & Passion Fruit Smoothie

Ingredients

- ½ Cup coconut cream
- ½ cup frozen blueberries
- ½ Cup passion fruit juice
- 1 tbsp chia seeds

Directions

1. Place all ingredients into a blender
2. Blend on high until smooth
3. Serve and enjoy

Strawberry, Mango & Coconut Smoothie

Ingredients
- 1 cup coconut milk beverage
- 1/2 cup frozen strawberries
- 1/2 cup frozen mango chunks
- 1 tablespoon coconut oil

Directions
1. Place all ingredients into a blender
2. Blend on high until smooth
3. Serve and enjoy

Refreshing Green

Ingredients

- 3 cups chopped romaine (or favorite green) ($1.00)
- 1 cup cubed pineapple, frozen ($2.00)
- 1 banana, sliced and frozen ($.20)
- 2 tablespoons lemon juice (optional) ($.20)
- 1 teaspoon vanilla ($.10)
- 1 cup water
- 10 ice cubes
- stevia to taste (optional)

Directions

1. Place all ingredients into a blender
2. Blend on high until smooth
3. Serve and enjoy

Vanilla, Pear Smoothie

Ingredients

- 1 cup raw spinach
- 3 ounces coconut cream
- 1 pear
- 1 kiwi, peeled
- 1/4 ripe avocado
- 1 cup frozen raspberries
- 1 tsp. vanilla
- 1/2 teaspoon flaxmeal
- 2 cups cold water

Directions

1. Place all ingredients into a blender
2. Blend on high until smooth
3. Serve and enjoy

Blueberry, Lime Smoothie

Ingredients
- 1 cup almond milk or coconut milk beverage
- 1 cup frozen blueberries
- 1/2 avocado
- Juice of 1 lime
- 1/2 teaspoon agave or maple syrup

Directions
1. Place all ingredients into a blender
2. Blend on high until smooth
3. Serve and enjoy

Pomegranate & Grapefruit Smoothie

Ingredients

- 1 Grapefruit
- 1/2 seeded pomegranate
- 1 banana
- 1 teaspoon of mixed seeds (preferably milled)

Directions

1. Place all ingredients into a blender
2. Blend on high until smooth
3. Serve and enjoy

Cardamom Berry Chia Smoothie

Ingredients

- 1 1/2 cups almond milk
- 3 tablespoons chia seeds
- 1 cup frozen raspberries
- 1/2 cup frozen strawberries
- 1 teaspoon ground cardamom

Directions

1. Soak Chia Seeds in 1 cup almond milk.
2. Let sit for 20 minutes.
3. Place all ingredients into a blender
4. Blend on high until smooth
5. Serve and enjoy

Dark Chocolate &Peanut Butter Smoothie

Ingredients

- 2 frozen bananas
- 2 Medjool dates, pitted
- 3 tbsp peanut butter
- 2 tbsp cacao powder
- 2 ¼ cups unsweetened almond milk
- Optional: 2 teaspoons lucuma powder

Directions

1. Place all ingredients into a blender
2. Blend on high until smooth
3. Serve and enjoy

Chapter 5:
Vegan Lifestyle Changes

Certainly you are now feeling motivated and ready to eat healthy Vegan foods which will help you achieve your ideal body and make a positive impact on the earth and all its' inhabitance. A lifestyle change that, I hope will be a good fit for you and that you will stick to from now henceforth.

However, it is important to note that lifestyle changes are a process that takes a lot of time getting used to and you therefore require support.

The fact that you are now ready to make a change is a huge step; the difficult part usually comes in committing and following through with your goals.

Here are a few tips that can set you on the right path of success.

Make a plan that you can follow through

Look at your plan as a road map that is supposed to guide you on this amazing journey of change. Don't stress too much about it. In fact, look at it like an adventure that is going to impact positively on your life.

Be specific with every plan you make and most of all, be realistic. If your plan is to lose weight; how much weight do you want to lose and within what time period?

Small but sure

The best way to meet your goals is to start small by setting daily goals then let these transform into weekly goals.

Drop one bad habit at a time, don't go cold turkey!

We acquire bad habits over the course of time and so does replacing them with healthy habits this is the surest way to success. Take it one habit after another until finally you start leading a pure Vegan way of life.

Exercise reigns!

Earlier on we saw that exercise is one of the best metabolism boosters. You also want to tone up your body after losing all that weight and what better way than using exercise to get some beautiful muscles?

The important thing is to choose a workout that works best for you. If you are a no pain no gain' kind of person, then weight lifting might just be the thing for you. If you love adventure, hiking, outdoor running, rock climbing and other outdoor exercises will work perfectly for you. If you love dancing, you can join Zumba classes and so on. Make sure you get a workout that you will be looking forward to going to and not one that you will be looking for excuses not to go to.

Most importantly...

Your body is a temple that deserves to be well taken care of and nourished. Make your health your priority and you will always make the right choices for your body.

The Vegan Diet is the epitome of how you should feed your body. Don't be too hard on yourself either if you slip. Just pick yourself up and resume from where you left of. With time you will find that you will no longer crave junk and over-processed food.

Your body will be so in tune with the Vegan Diet you will only want to eat what you are sure is providing positive nutrition to your body.

It's time to make the big Vegan change!

Conclusion

Thank you again for purchasing this book!

I hope this book was able to help you understand the premise of the vegan diet, why we need to save our animals and our planet and most of all, why the vegan diet is just what you need to steer your health in the right direction.

The next step is to jump right into the diet by making healthy and smart vegan food choices to ensure you meet your recommended daily nutrition. If you are starting out on veganism, you should join an online vegan group that will further guide you on the best way to take up the vegan diet and tips and tricks to stay on the diet.

We have seen the immense health benefits of the vegan diet. Combine it with regular exercise, clean water and healthy habits and you will discover the fountain of health and youth.

Finally, if you feel that you have received any value from this book, then I'd like to ask you for a favor, would you be kind enough to leave a review for on Amazon? It'd be greatly appreciated!

Made in the USA
Middletown, DE
13 July 2018